THOMAS CARLYLE

HOW TO KNOW HIM

By

BLISS PERRY

Author of

A STUDY OF PROSE FICTION, THE AMATEUR SPIRIT
WALT WHITMAN, ETC., ETC.

WITH PORTRAIT

INDIANAPOLIS
THE BOBBS-MERRILL COMPANY
PUBLISHERS

PRESS OF
BRAUNWORTH & CO.
BOOKBINDERS AND PRINTERS
BROOKLYN, N. Y.

PRELIMINARY

Thomas Carlyle was a Scottish peasant who became one of the great names of English literature. The story of that transformation and achievement has been told and retold by many a brilliant writer during the generation which has elapsed since Carlyle's death.

No record of personal development and literary accomplishment is more fascinating. Yet it is not the aim of this book to present one more biography of Carlyle. It is rather to exhibit, as far as possible in Carlyle's own words, the working of his mind. His books are intensely, supremely personal. They review his own struggles, his slowly-won mastery over himself and his circumstances, his entire theory of human life and conduct. With a vividness almost if not quite unrivalled in the whole history of literature, they describe his ancestry and early environment, his unsystematic education, his painful quest of a career, and the spiritual conflicts by which he came to an ultimate command of himself. This main battle once won, he perfected, between the ages of thirty and thirty-five, his theory of biography and history. It remained essentially unchanged throughout the rest of his long life. His epoch-making histories—*The French Revolution, Cromwell's Letters and Speeches,* and *Frederick the Great*—are the endeavors of an extraordinary literary artist to adjust this theory to the facts of a vanished European society. His social and political writings—like *Chartism, Past and Present,* and *Latter-Day Pamphlets*—apply his theory, as a surgeon applies his knife and caustic, to the ills of the England of his day. Carlyle the critic of books, Carlyle the biographer and historian of great men and great events, Carlyle the prophet and mystic, are thus essentially and radically one. To disbelieve this message or "gospel" of Carlyle is quite within the rights of any contemporary reader, but there is no longer any excuse for misunderstanding it. The present book is merely a fresh attempt to let Carlyle explain himself and his views, as adequately as the inexorable count of pages will permit. We must allow this prince of talkers to do almost all the talking; but before he begins we must say a word about his Scotch accent—the rich accent of Annandale.

B. P.

CONTENTS

CARLYLE

CARLYLE

CHAPTER I

THE HERITAGE

TRAMPING into Ecclefechan one bright August morning with the village postman, I remarked that most books about Carlyle gave the impression that he was born in a dreary and unattractive place.

"'Tis the sweetest spot in all Dumfriesshire," said the postman loyally; and indeed it was sweet enough,—a fine rolling country, with rich woodlands and yellowing grain, and bright streams foaming down to the Solway. The straggling village, a Border town sixteen miles beyond Carlisle, on the Great North Road from London to Glasgow, has changed but little since Thomas Carlyle first opened his eyes in the upper chamber of the stone-arch house in 1795. The tiny stream still flows through the village street. A few rods from the house where Carlyle was born is the churchyard where he was buried, on that grim winter day of 1881. The caretaker of the "arch-house" will show you the relics, and confess that all that she and the other village children knew about Carlyle, in the height of his fame, was that an old man was wont to visit Ecclefechan every summer and that the children would say: "I see old Tom Caerl is back." The guardian of the churchyard, an old woman, shrugs her shoulders at your comment upon the neglect of the grave. "I expect they'll be saving the money," is her Scotch explanation; and the ghost of the dead man gives, very possibly, an ironic chuckle.

The whole country-side is full of ghosts, indeed, to the lover of Carlyle. Six miles to the south of Ecclefechan, on the Solway, lies Annan,—whither the little fellow trudged off to school in 1806, his father by his side. To the northeast and north lie the farms of Scotsbrig and Mainhill. Farther toward the northeast is Dumfries, and beyond Dumfries, on the moors, are Templand and Craigenputtoch. The unlucky reader to whom, as yet, these names are only names, should steep himself without delay in Carlyle's *Reminiscences,* and particularly in the first chapter, written in the week after his father's death in 1832. There is the unforgetable portrait of James Carlyle, stone-mason, descended from a line of Borderers:—"pithy, bitter-speaking bodies and awfu' fighters,"—himself an austere man with deep inner springs of tenderness, who taught his gifted son the power of phrase and the gospel of work. "It was he *exclusively* that determined on *educating* me; that from his small hard-earned funds sent me to school and college and made me whatever I am or may become. . . . He was a man of perhaps the very largest natural endowment of any it has been my lot to converse with. None of us will forget that bold glowing style of his, flowing free from his untutored soul, full of metaphors (though he knew not what a metaphor was) with all manner of potent words which he appropriated and applied with a surprising accuracy you often would not guess whence—brief, energetic, and which I should say conveyed the most perfect picture, definite, clear, not in ambitious colours but in full white sunlight, of all the dialects I have ever listened to. Nothing did I ever hear him undertake to render visible which did not become almost ocularly so. Never shall we again hear such speech as that was. The whole district knew of it and laughed joyfully over it, not knowing how otherwise to express the feeling it gave them; emphatic I have heard him beyond all men. In anger he had no need of oaths, his words were like sharp arrows that smote into the very heart. The fault was that he exaggerated (which tendency I also inherit), yet only in description and for the sake chiefly of humourous effect. He was a man of rigid, even scrupulous veracity. I have often heard him turn back when he thought his strong words were misleading, and correct them into mensurative accuracy. . . . This great maxim of philosophy he had gathered by the teaching of nature alone—that man was created to work—not to speculate, or feel, or dream. Accordingly he set his whole heart thitherwards. He did work wisely and unweariedly (*Ohne Hast aber ohne Rast*) and perhaps performed more with the tools he had than any man I now know. It should have made me sadder than it did to hear the young ones sometimes complaining of his slow punctuality and thoroughness. He would leave nothing till it was done. . . . On the whole ought I not to rejoice that God was pleased to give me such a father; that from earliest years I had the example of a real Man of God's own making continually before me? Let me learn of *him*. Let me write my books as he built his houses, and walk as blamelessly through this shadow world; if God so will, to rejoin him at last. Amen."

Of Carlyle's mother, Margaret Aitken, the stonemason's second wife, there is no full-length description in the *Reminiscences,* but from the family letters it is easy to perceive what manner of person she was,—an affectionate, yearning, solicitous woman, loyal like all the Carlyle clan, and unspeakably proud of Tom. She learned painfully to write, in middle age, so that she might correspond with him; she tried to understand his books, and surely when, with his literary glory fairly won, son and mother sat smoking pipes together on her doorstep in the late-lingering Scottish twilights, she understood him and was happy. One and all, and until the very end of their long lives, the Carlyles were bound together by a fierce and sweet family affection. Thomas and John, the two educated sons, put money in their purses at last, but even when they were poorest, some shillings out of every hard-won pound went freely to the less fortunate of the clan.

Their religious heritage was Dissent. James Carlyle belonged to the sect of Burgher-Seceders, or "New Lichts." "A man who awoke to the belief that he actually had a soul to be saved or lost was apt to be found among the Dissenting people, and to have given up attendance on the Kirk," says Thomas. "Very remarkable are those old Seceder clergy to me now when I look back on them. Most of the chief figures among them in Irving's time and mine were hoary old men; men so like what one might call antique Evangelists in ruder vesture and 'poor scholars and gentlemen of Christ,' I have nowhere met with in monasteries or churches, among Protestant or Papal clergy, in any country of the world." It was among these gray heads in the Ecclefechan meeting-house—"that poor temple of my childhood"—that Carlyle first learned that sacred lesson of Reverence which he afterward discovered in *Wilhelm Meister*. The wish and intention of his father and mother was that he should fit himself for the ministry. It was with this aim that the minister of the meeting-house first taught him Latin, as a preparation for Annan grammar school and the University of Edinburgh. This dream of a consecrated calling faded slowly, to his father's

silent bewilderment and his mother's keen sorrow,
but Carlyle never lost his sense of dedication to the
highest things. He remained to the end, like Emerson, but far more deeply than Emerson, a child of
Calvinism, rejecting its formulas, but faithful to
its mandates to the soul.

The law of Carlyle's childhood, then, was the
old rule of poverty, chastity and obedience; of family love and loyalty; the hard, narrow and vital experience of a country-bred boy; and the provincial,
racial stamp of the Scottish Border, with its rude
face and its inner flashing pride.

CHAPTER II

THE MAKING OF THE MAN

THE authentic facts as to Carlyle's education are found in the *Reminiscences*—particularly in the chapter on Irving—and in his *Early Letters*. He came but slowly and painfully to the finding of himself and his true path. The two years at Annan were wretched. The four years at Edinburgh, from his fifteenth to his nineteenth year, were not unlike the experience of most Scottish youth of his period. His satirical picture of the University in *Sartor Resartus* does scant justice to his own teachers, who were reputable, though not highly distinguished scholars. He was well nourished upon farm supplies from Ecclefechan, and he had no real troubles except "growing pains." He made warm friendships. His Latin and French were good, and his mathematics brilliant; he learned little or no Greek, and art and science remained—as always—a sealed book to him. After four winters as "student in

arts," he left Edinburgh, without a degree, but en-
rolled as a student of divinity, with the duty of
making an annual report of progress and handing
in an essay. He had won the appointment of math-
ematical tutor in his old school, Annan Academy.
Two discontented years here were followed by two
years of private tutoring at Kirkcaldy, where Irving
lent him books. He now abandoned the preparation for the ministry, and ended by taking private
pupils in Edinburgh for four years more,—meanwhile reading law a little, studying mineralogy, mas-
tering German, and writing some hack articles for
Brewster's *Edinburgh Encyclopedia.*

He was "drifting" in these years, much as Thackeray, Tennyson and Walt Whitman drifted in their
turn, until they found their bearings. Carlyle found
his, toward the end of his Edinburgh tutoring, in the
famous Leith Walk "Conversion," recorded in the
"Everlasting No" chapter of *Sartor Resartus.* He
had denied, in that moment of fierce insight, that the
Devil—(*'der Geist der stets verneint'*) the Great
Denier, ruled his soul; and henceforward he was a
free man. A tutorship in the Buller family (1822-
1824) left him leisure for enormous reading, chiefly
in German literature, and for writing his first book,

the *Life of Schiller.* He visited London, where his friend Irving had become a fashionable preacher. He made a brief, but to him most valuable, trip to Paris. At a farm-house on Haddon Hill near his father's new farm at Mainhill, in the summer of 1825, he had the experience recorded in the "Everlasting Yea" chapter of *Sartor Resartus,*—the ecstatic moment of acceptance of the universe as God's world.

"I lived very silent, diligent, had long solitary rides (on my wild Irish horse Larry, good for the dietetic part), my meditatings, musings, and reflectings were continual; my thoughts went wandering (or travelling) through eternity, through time, and through space, so far as poor I had scanned or known, and were now to my endless solacement coming back with tidings to me! This year I found that I had conquered all my scepticisms, agonising doubtings, fearful wrestlings with the foul and vile and soul-murdering Mud-gods of my epoch; had escaped as from a worse than Tartarus, with all its Phlegethons and Stygian quagmires, and was emerging free in spirit into the eternal blue of the ether, where, blessed be heaven! I have for the spiritual part ever since lived, looking down upon the welter-

ings of my poor fellow-mortals, in such multitudes
and millions still stuck in that fatal element, and
have had no concern whatever in their Puseyisms,
ritualisms, metaphysical controversies and cob-
webberies, and no feeling of my own except honest
silent pity for the serious or religious part of them,
and occasional indignation, for the poor world's
sake, at the frivolous secular and impious part, with
their universal suffrages, their Nigger emancipa-
tions, sluggard and scoundrel Protection societies,
and 'unexampled prosperities' for the time being!
What my pious joy and gratitude then was, let the
pious soul figure.   In a fine and veritable sense, I,
poor, obscure, without outlook, almost without
worldly hope, had become independent of the world.
What was death itself, from the world, to what I
had come through?   I understood well what the old
Christian people meant by *conversion*, by God's infinite mercy to them.   I had, in effect, gained an immense victory, and for a number of years had, in
spite of nerves and chagrins, a constant inward happiness that was quite royal and supreme, in which
all temporal evil was transient and insignificant, and
which essentially remains with me still, though far
oftener *eclipsed* and lying deeper *down* than then.

Once more, thank Heaven for its highest gift. I then felt, and still feel, endlessly indebted to Goethe in the business. He, in his fashion, I perceived, had travelled the steep rocky road before me, the first of the moderns." . . .

He had already begun to correspond with Goethe. But there is another series of letters, far more significant even than the Goethe correspondence, in revealing the character of the young Carlyle. In May, 1821, he had been introduced by Irving to Miss Jane Welsh of Haddington, and had promptly fallen in love with this brilliant and ambitious girl. *The Love Letters of Thomas Carlyle and Jane Welsh* are among the most veracious and illuminating documents of the crucial period of Carlyle's life. His unselfishness of spirit, wide-ranging play of intellect, and nobleness of aspiration, are revealed throughout. No wonder that she wrote to a woman friend, when all the occasional misunderstandings and reluctances of her engagement drew to a close: "He possesses all the qualities I deem essential in *my* Husband, a warm true heart to love me, a towering intellect to command me, and a spirit of fire to be the guiding star of my life." . . .

They were married in 1826, and after two winters in Edinburgh, where Carlyle was occupied with writing articles for the Reviews, they removed to the Welsh's farm-house by Craigenputtoch—the "Hill of the Hawks"—on the moorland north of Dumfries.

In the six solitary years at Craigenputtoch—1828 to 1834—broken indeed by long visits to London and Edinburgh—Carlyle grew to his full mental stature.

Mrs. Carlyle, always delicate in health, profited by the keen moorland air and the long rides on horseback. Housekeeping, in that remote district, brought its natural trials, but occasionally they had charming guests, like Jeffrey and Emerson, ("our quiet night of clear fine talk"), and they enjoyed unburdened leisure for reading and writing. "We had trouble with servants, with many paltry elements and objects, and were very poor; but I do not think our days were sad, and certainly not hers in especial, but mine rather. We read together at night, one winter, through 'Don Quixote' in the original; Tasso in ditto had come before; but that did not last very long. I was diligently writing and reading there; wrote most of the 'Miscellanies' there, for Foreign, Edinburgh, etc., Reviews (obliged to keep several strings to my bow), and took serious thought about every part of every one of them. After finishing an article, we used to get on horseback, or mount into our soft old rig, and drive away, either to her mother's (Templand, fourteen miles off), or to my father and mother's (Scotsbrig, seven or six-and-thirty miles); the pleasantest journeys I ever made, and the pleasantest visits. Stay perhaps three days; hardly ever more than four; then back to work and silence . . . We were not unhappy at Craigenputtoch; perhaps these were our happiest days. Useful, continual labour, essentially successful; that makes even the moor green. I found I could do fully twice as much work in a given time there, as with my best effort was possible in London, such the interruptions, etc. Once, in the winter time, I remember counting that for three months, there had not been any stranger, not even a beggar, called at Craigenputtoch door."

The intellectual results of the Craigenputtoch period were threefold. Here Carlyle brought to an end his critical studies of German literature, developed his own theory of biography and history (which was also capable of being turned into a theory of conduct), and made in *Count Cagliostro* and *The Diamond Necklace* his preparatory studies for *The French Revolution.* *Sartor Resartus,* which was completed in 1831, precisely midway in the Craigenputtoch epoch, has been described as a mountain pool draining the great upland of German literature.   But it is also a personal document of the highest significance in revealing the manner of man Carlyle had become.   "It was the best I had in me," he said stoically when the three London publishers, Fraser, Longman and Murray, had in turn rejected the manuscript, and Carlyle had tied it up and laid it away in a box.   "I did my best," and Craigenputtoch had likewise done its best for him, and he had to choose between going on to London and its fuller life, or remaining a mere provincial figure. The German studies, continued now for ten years, had taught him many things.   He had become the foremost British authority in that field, and though he never completed his outlined *History of German Literature,* nor even began his projected *Life of Luther*—for him a far better subject than *Frederick*—his critical essays upon Schiller and Goethe, Novalis and Richter, and the other German philosophers and poets have remained one of the enduring treasures of our own literature.   Slowly he turned from eighteenth century Germany to eighteenth century France—a more natural field for a Scotchman, since the Scottish type of education had been, since the days of Queen Mary, largely French,—and revealed in his essays upon Diderot and Voltaire an astonishing familiarity with the ways of the Old Régime. But his "trial flights" as a story-teller of the Pre-Revolutionary epoch taught him that the books essential for a history of the Revolution itself were not then accessible in Scotland; and thus this road, too, led to London.

But the valuable literary lesson of the Craigenputtoch exile, after all, is as clearly written in Carlyle's essays on Burns and Johnson, and on History and Biography, as it is in any of his studies of European events or European figures. This lesson, which we must presently examine in his own words, is the cardinal point of his creed as an historian and biographer: namely, that all art of portrayal depends upon preliminary imaginative insight, and that the secret of insight is sympathy. To find your man, to love him, then to paint him as he is: this is the law—Carlyle thought—for all truly creative work in biography and history. London, in 1834, was slow to believe it.

CHAPTER III

N O private house in London is so well known to Americans as 24 Cheyne Row, Chelsea, where Carlyle lived from 1834 until his death in 1881. "Chelsea," he wrote his wife, who had remained in Scotland while he was househunting, "is a singular heterogeneous kind of a spot, very dirty and confused in some places, quite beautiful in others, abounding with antiquities and the traces of great men—Sir Thomas More, Steele, Smollett, etc. Our row, which for the last three doors or so is a street, and none of the noblest, runs out upon a 'Parade' (perhaps they call it) running along the shore of the river, a broad highway with large shady trees, boats lying moored, and a smell of shipping and tan." A letter to his mother is no less picturesque: "We lie safe at a bend of the river, away from all the great roads, have air and quiet hardly inferior to Craigenputtoch, an outlook from the

17

back windows into mere leafy regions with here and there a red high-peaked old roof looking through; and see nothing of London, except by day the summits of St. Paul's Cathedral and Westminster Abbey, and by night the gleam of the great Babylon affronting the peaceful skies. The house itself is probably the best we have ever lived in—a right old, strong, roomy brick house, built near one hundred fifty years ago, and likely to see three races of these modern fashionables fall before it comes down."

This brick house,—now a Carlyle museum, rich in relics and in memories,—sheltered as strange and brilliant a man and woman as were to be found in London. Carlyle was now thirty-nine: noticeably tall, with touzled black hair, wonderful violet-blue eyes, and the fresh red cheeks of a peasant. His wife was six years younger: a fascinating, self-willed creature, endowed with brains, beauty and a tongue. Like her husband, she suffered from chronic dyspepsia; like him, she was proud, sensitive, affectionate in a Spartan fashion, and a fiery Scot. They were both aliens in London, as the Scotch have ever been; and they conquered their London in due time, as the Scotch are wont to do. Finely loyal to each other in all essential ways, there

was in each an overlying vein of hardness, more
pronounced in the wife than in the husband. The
tenderness which each felt often remained unuttered.
"Only think of my husband having given me a little
present!" Mrs. Carlyle wrote in 1842; "he who
never attends to such nonsense as birthdays. . . .
I can not tell you how *wae* his little gift made me,
as well as glad; it was the first thing of the kind he
ever gave me in his life. In great matters he is always kind and considerate; but these little attentions,
which we women attach so much importance to, he
was never in the habit of rendering to any one; his
up-bringing, and the severe turn of mind he has
from nature, had alike indisposed him toward them."
Their marriage was, to their disappointment, child-
less.

As the years of fierce intellectual labor went
by, Carlyle grew increasingly preoccupied with his
tasks; though he did not realize how completely
they had absorbed him until the tragic clearness of
self-examination, in the solitary years following his
wife's death, revealed his error when it was too late.
Mrs. Carlyle had her own circle of friends and admirers, and though she renounced—no doubt with
wisdom—the literary ambitions which had dom-

inated her girlhood, she led her own intellectual
life, with sympathies and antipathies which her husband did not share. To think, however, of their
marriage as an unhappy one, is to do it less than
justice. Neither the husband nor the wife was of a
"happy" temperament; both were nervous invalids,
thin-skinned and unreasonable and equipped with
biting tongues; but, all things considered, it would
have been difficult to discover in all London a better
mate for either of them. Tennyson's robust com-
mon-sense judgment has often been quoted: "Mr.
and Mrs. Carlyle on the whole enjoyed life together,
else they would not have chaffed one another so
heartily."

The story of Carlyle's life in London has been
told with consummate art by Froude, and far more
briefly and with greater justice by Richard Garnett.
As a record of the production of books, it is a tale
of triumph after triumph. It will be remembered
that Carlyle's only writings, up to 1834, had been
the *Life of Schiller,* some translations from the German,—of which Goethe's *Wilhelm Meister* was the
most significant,—reviews and articles and essays,
and *Sartor Resartus,* which had been printed as a

serial in *Fraser's,* but which no publisher had the
courage to issue as a book. His first task in London, attempted with the encouragement and help of
John Stuart Mill, was *The History of the French
Revolution.* This astounding performance, whose
method and technique must be the subject of later
comment, was published in 1837. It marked Carlyle, at once, as one of the greatest writers of his
epoch. *Sartor Resartus,* first printed in book form
in Boston in 1836, under Emerson's supervision,
was now reissued in London (1838), and it was
followed in the next year by a collection of *Critical
and Miscellaneous Essays* in four volumes. Then
came *Chartism,* and the brilliant London lectures on
Heroes and Hero-Worship, delivered to notable audiences in 1840, and printed, after revision, in 1841.
Carlyle was already busy with one of his most
gigantic tasks, a life of Cromwell, which ultimately
restricted itself to an annotated edition of Cromwell's *Letters and Speeches,* published in 1845. He
had paused, in a kind of rage over the social conditions of England, two years before, to paint the
contrasting pictures of *Past and Present.* In 1850
came the furious *Latter-Day Pamphlets* denouncing
the age in which he lived; yet in 1851 this was fol-

lowed by one of Carlyle's most quiet and perfect performances in pure literature, *The Life of Sterling*. Five or six years earlier than this, he had begun to read in preparation for the last and most difficult of his Herculean labors, *The History of Frederick the Great*. The first two volumes appeared in 1858. The last page of the sixth and final volume was written in January, 1865. "Sunday night, January 5, 1865, went out to post-office with my last leaf of 'Frederick' MS. Evening still vivid to me. I was not joyful of mood; sad rather, mournfully thankful, but indeed half killed, and utterly wearing out and sinking into stupefied collapse after my 'comatose' efforts to continue the long flight of thirteen years to finis. On her face, too, when I went out, there was a silent, faint, and pathetic smile, which I well felt at the moment, and better now! Often enough had it cut me to the heart to think what she was suffering by this book, in which she had no share, no interest, nor any word at all; and with what noble and perfect constancy of silence she bore it all. My own heroic little woman!"

It was in the following spring of 1866 that Carlyle, now a tired old man of seventy-one, elected

Lord Rector of his own University of Edinburgh by a large majority over his opponent Disraeli, delivered his last public utterance, the noble and touching *Edinburgh Address.* It was a day of boundless triumph, won among his own people; but before he could return to London he was stricken with the tidings of Mrs. Carlyle's sudden death. She had never been more proud of him nor more fond of him than in that high moment. "It seems so long," she wrote in her last letter, "since you went away."

"By the calamity of April last," Carlyle wrote to Emerson in the following January, "I lost my little all in this world; and have no soul left who can make any corner of this world into a home for me any more. Bright, heroic, tender, true and noble was that lost treasure of my heart, who faithfully accompanied me in all the rocky ways and climbings; and I am forever poor without her. She was snatched from me in a moment,—as by a death from the gods. Very beautiful her death was; radiantly beautiful (to those who understood it) had all her life been: *quid plura?* I should be among the dullest and stupidest, if I were not among the saddest of all men. But not a word more on all this."

CHAPTER IV

SOLITUDE

CARLYLE survived his wife fifteen years: a solitary, broken figure of a man, familiar to the world in Whistler's portrait. But the truth is that he had always been solitary in spirit: "infinitely solitary," as he had written to Emerson in 1852. Emerson's tests of capacity for friendship, it may be remembered, were truth, tenderness, and the ability to do without friendship. Carlyle possessed these qualifications to a singular degree. His rough sincerity, his deep wells of tenderness, his passionate family affection, characterize him from first to last. He seems to have had no warm friends in childhood, but he won them in college, and held them throughout the long years when he was seeking his true career. His friendliness of disposition is proved by his correspondence with Irving, Emerson, Sterling and Mill; and by his intercourse with his London neighbors like the Hunts and the Gilchrists. He had admiring acquaintances in every walk of life: aristocrats like Milnes and the Ashburtons, Radicals like the Bullers, Mazzini and John Forster, churchmen like Thirlwall and Wilberforce, men of science like Tyndall and Huxley, men of letters like Tennyson, Fitzgerald, Browning, Thackeray, Ruskin, Norton, counted themselves among his intimates. But they all knew well enough that in the recesses of his soul he dwelt apart. It was his nature, and he was incapable of change. More than most men, he had a sense of what Swift called the transiency and vanity of all earthly things. With Andrew Marvell he could say:

> "At my back I always hear
> Time's winged chariot hurrying near."

He wrote in his Journal for 1854: "Time! Death! All-devouring Time! This thought *'Exeunt omnes,'* and how the generations are like crops of grass, *temporary,* very, and all *vanishes,* as it were an apparition and a ghost: these things, though half a century old in me, possess my mind as they never did before." Many of Carlyle's sublimest passages in *Sartor* and elsewhere, sound this note of transiency: "Time's winged chariot hurrying near," perceived by the supersensitive ear of a solitary.

His literary work was essentially done, when the final loneliness began in 1866. It lasted until his death in 1881. In the first shock of his bereavement he spent his days in meditation upon the happiness that had been so close to him while he had been too often unaware of it. With meditation there was swiftly mingled a passionate regret for all his blindness to the little things that make up the sum of a woman's happiness, and he reproached himself bitterly, now that it was too late. He set himself to the mournful task of writing a memoir of his wife, and then of annotating her letters, in heart-broken phrases which reveal all his old literary power, but which were tempered by no restraint. This memoir, and the *Letters and Memorials of Jane Welsh Carlyle,* prepared in tragic expiation of a guilt of blindness which few persons would have been cruel enough to impute to him, became after his death, and through the deliberate choice of his executor, Froude, a scourge to Carlyle's memory.

In all outward ways, the old man's closing years were tranquil. The income from his books had long been larger than the frugal life of Chelsea demanded, leaving a generous margin for charities. His niece Mary Aitken, afterward Mrs. Alexander

Carlyle, kept house for him. The stream of disciples and friends still flowed without cessation toward Cheyne Row. Germany conferred upon him the splendid order *Pour le Merite*, founded by his hero Frederick, and Queen Victoria, through her premier Disraeli, offered him the Grand Cross of the Bath. His eightieth birthday, in 1875, was commemorated by a gold medal and an address signed by more than one hundred of the foremost names in Great Britain. Slowly he lost strength, thereafter, though his spirit did not pass until February 5, 1881. It had been known for weeks that he was dying, and the words that Walt Whitman wrote in his Camden diary will remind some Americans of their own emotions in that hour:

". . . In the fine cold night, unusually clear, (February 5, '81) as I walked some open grounds adjacent, the condition of Carlyle, and his approaching—perhaps even then actual—death, filled me with thoughts eluding statement, and curiously blending with the scene. The planet Venus, an hour high in the west, with all her volume and lustre recover'd, (she has been shorn and languid for nearly a year,) including an additional sentiment I never noticed before—not merely voluptuous, Paphian,

steeping, fascinating—now with calm commanding
seriousness and hauteur—the Milo Venus now. Up-
ward to the zenith, Jupiter, Saturn, and the moon
past her quarter, trailing in procession, with the
Pleiades following, and the constellation Taurus,
and red Aldebaran. Not a cloud in heaven. Orion
strode through the southeast, with his glittering
belt—and a trifle below hung the sun of the night,
Sirius. Every star dilated, more vitreous, nearer
than usual. Not as in some clear nights when the
larger stars entirely outshine the rest. Every little
star or cluster just as distinctly visible, and just as
nigh. Berenice's hair showing every gem, and new
ones. To the northeast and north the Sickle, the
Goat and kids, Cassiopeia, Castor and Pollux, and
the two Dippers. While through the whole of this
silent indescribable show, inclosing and bathing my
whole receptivity, ran the thought of Carlyle dying.
(To soothe and spiritualize, and, as far as may be,
solve the mysteries of death and genius, consider
them under the stars at midnight.)

"And now that he has gone hence, can it be that
Thomas Carlyle, soon to chemically dissolve in ashes
and by winds, remains an identity still? In ways
perhaps eluding all the statements, lore and specula-

tions of ten thousand years—eluding all possible statements to mortal sense—does he yet exist, a definite, vital being, a spirit, an individual—perhaps now wafted in space among those stellar systems, which, suggestive and limitless as they are, merely edge more limitless, far more suggestive systems? I have no doubt of it. In silence, of a fine night, such questions are answer'd to the soul, the best answers that can be given. With me, too, when depress'd by some specially sad event, or tearing problem, I wait till I go out under the stars for the last voiceless satisfaction."

Carlyle was buried in Ecclefechan on that "cold dreary February morning" so touchingly described by Froude.

CHAPTER V

SOON the storm of detraction broke. The blame for it lies fairly on the shoulders of James Anthony Froude, Carlyle's friend and literary executor. But Froude's action was not so much a betrayal of a trust—as has been bitterly asseverated—as it was an error of judgment: error in reading the characters of both Mr. and Mrs. Carlyle, error in interpreting Carlyle's wishes, error in artistic presentation of the outstanding features of his personality.

The facts must be briefly stated here. Carlyle's original executors were his brother, Doctor John Carlyle, the Dante scholar, and John Forster. After Forster's death, Froude's name was substituted for his, in 1878. John Carlyle died in 1879, two years before his brother. In 1881, then, Froude had the responsibility of deciding what manuscript remains of Thomas Carlyle should be published. Ten years earlier Carlyle had placed in Froude's hands a collection of manuscripts, including the memoir of Mrs. Carlyle written immediately after her death, memoirs of Irving and Jeffrey, notes upon Wordsworth and Southey, and a sketch of Carlyle's father written after his death in 1832. This material Froude decided to issue as Carlyle's *Reminiscences*. He stated clearly in the preface that "perhaps most of it was not intended for publication." But he did not print the solemn injunction which Carlyle had written at the end of the manuscript volume: "I still mainly mean to burn this book before my own departure, but feel that I shall always have a kind of grudge to do it, and an indolent excuse, 'Not yet; wait, any day that can be done!' and then it is possible the thing may be left behind me, legible to interested survivors—friends only. I will hope, and with worthy curiosity, not unworthy! In which event, I solemnly forbid them, each and all, to publish this bit of writing as it stands here; and warn them that without fit editing no part of it should be printed (nor so far as I can order shall ever be); and that the editing of perhaps nine-tenths of it will, after I am gone, have become impossible. *T. C., 28 July, 1866.*"

Froude's omission of this postscript was a grave
error of judgment, as it proved, although he unquestionably supposed that Carlyle had changed his
mind about the matter, and that Carlyle's verbal
directions to him, authorizing him to use his dis-
cretion, when the manuscripts were given to his
keeping in 1871, superseded the postscript of 1866.
To have stated this with frankness, would have been
Froude's wiser course. But he could not have an-
ticipated the violence of the criticism provoked by
the publication of these intimate records of Carlyle's impressions of his contemporaries. It is likely
that Carlyle himself never recognized how blistering
his own words were. In private talk his extreme
expressions were often accompanied by a hearty hu-
morous laugh at his own extravagance of speech,
and the laugh corrected and humanized the total impression made upon his hearers. But now, in 1881,
the readers of the *Reminiscences* could not hear the
dead man's delighted chuckle at his hyperboles; they
felt the harshness, the vindictiveness of Carlyle's
attitude toward many honored names, and they
blamed Froude for these improprieties. The painful impression as to Carlyle's true nature was increased by Froude's publication of *The Letters and*

Memorials of Jane Welsh Carlyle, prepared, as we have seen, in the husband's agony of sorrow and contrition, and surely not intended by him to be given unrevised to the eye of the great public. These books were soon accompanied by Froude's massive *Life of Carlyle,* in four volumes: a superb and enduring monument to his hero, and nevertheless a biography whose immediate and obvious influence was to emphasize certain flaws in Carlyle's character.

In the light of facts subsequently revealed, it is now certain that Froude's admiration for Mrs. Carlyle and his chivalrous desire to present her as a woman "misunderstood"—even by her husband— led him into exaggeration. He overestimated her sacrifice "of ambition and fortune" in marrying him. Jane Welsh did not possess the social station, nor the property, and it is fairly clear that she did not possess the original intellectual force, which Froude attributed to her. What was far more sinister than this, he magnified her very natural jealousy of Carlyle's friendship for the first Lady Ashburton in such a way as to make many readers of the biography imagine that Carlyle was guilty, not merely of wilful cruelty leading to estrangement, but of actual infidelity. All this seems absurd enough now, but the immediate result was to deal Carlyle's personal character a blow from which it was not easy to recover. Was not Froude a close friend, the possessor of thousands of letters and other manuscript documents, and was he not among the most eminent of historians, skilled in collecting and weighing evidence? The most loyal of Carlyle's admirers felt a sinking of the heart.

Very slowly the scales of public opinion began to turn. The Alexander Carlyles, greatly offended by Froude's methods, regained possession of the original manuscripts utilized by the literary executor. Charles Eliot Norton now had access to them, and in a vigorous article in the *New Princeton Review* (July, 1886) exposed Froude's characteristic carelessness and inaccuracy in dealing with manuscript sources, particularly with regard to the *Reminiscences*. Norton also edited Carlyle's correspondence with Emerson and with Goethe, and his early letters. Here was evidence as to Carlyle's real nature, not to be gainsaid. Then, twenty years after the first storm, appeared a series of volumes which cleared the air. In 1903 Mr. Alexander Carlyle printed the *New Letters and Memorials of Jane*

Welsh Carlyle, with an introduction by Sir James Crichton-Browne, setting forth Froude's defects as a biographer. Froude replied in his *My Relations with Carlyle* (1903). Crichton-Browne made a rejoinder in *The Nemesis of Froude* (1903), to which Froude, who died in 1904, did not reply. In that year Alexander Carlyle issued the *New Letters of Thomas Carlyle,* and in 1909 *The Love Letters of Thomas Carlyle and Jane Welsh.* The complete facts were at last made manifest, and Froude's brilliant and somewhat misleading "Life" of his hero stands corrected at the points where the unwary reader needed to be put upon his guard. Save for these defects arising from partiality of vision and artistic exaggeration, Froude's masterly performances will not be superseded.

CHAPTER VI

IT REMAINS to be said that a new generation of readers must find its own methods of approach to Carlyle. None of the great Victorian writers like Thackeray, Dickens, Newman, Ruskin, can be read by an American in the second decade of the twentieth century as they were read by their contemporaries. No vividness of historical imagination can transport us completely backward into that bygone epoch. Its literary, social and ethical atmosphere can not be reproduced. Much of the present reaction against the Early and Middle Victorians is stupid: it is what Doctor Johnson would call "pure ignorance." But some of it is the result of inevitable social change. Even during the forty years of Carlyle's living activity in the world of letters, there were profound alterations in the structure of English thought and in the conditions of English society. In 1832 he stood, or thought he stood, by the side of John Stuart Mill, the Radical; but they parted forever over the question of American slavery, and Carlyle stood frankly, in the eighteen-sixties, for the program of the "beneficent whip." This cost him the allegiance of many American admirers, and his tardy admission, after the close of the Civil War, that he might have been mistaken as to its real issue, left his general attitude toward democracy and liberty unchanged. He distrusted both. Anticipating Ruskin in his advocacy of popular education and of many social and administrative reforms, Carlyle would nevertheless be as disgruntled by the program of contemporary British Liberalism as he was by the Liberalism of the eighteen-forties. He would dislike no less the forward movements of contemporary thought in the United States. What then are we to search for in the twenty-five volumes of this typical mid-Victorian, most of whose work was finished—and by many, even then, thought antiquated—more than half a century ago? What go we out again into this wilderness to see?

Well, we shall see first of all a literary artist, a master of word and phrase. An eccentric, a "barbarian," a gesticulator, a lover of the extravagant

and the grotesque, Carlyle was nevertheless one of
the most cunning and effective workmen who have
wrought in the medium of human speech. He knew
precisely what he was doing, and he liked to ex-
pound the secrets of his profession. As realist, hu-
morist, portrait painter and story-teller, his place
is with the very greatest of men of letters, and he
won that place by understanding himself and his
task, and by following what was, for him, precisely
the right method. To watch this artist at his work
is to learn something of the immutable laws of
literature.

It may well be granted that Carlyle's eye and hand
are marvellous, but how about his mind? What
are his leading ideas? What is the ethical validity
of his famous gospels of "work" and of "sincerity"?
What is the philosophical value of his mysticism,
of the transcendental significance which he gives
to the terms "silence" and "nature of things"? What
shall be said to-day of his political views, his theory
of the "hero," his diagnosis of the "condition of
England," and the social remedies which he pro-
poses? Has he trust in progress, in the education
of the race? Does he believe that a democracy develops leadership or promotes fellowship? With

the word "faith" so often upon his eloquent lips, has he himself a living faith in man and in God, and in the co-operation of man with God?

It is the problem of this book to answer these questions if possible, and to answer them as far as possible in Carlyle's own words. The task will justify itself as we proceed, and perhaps there is no need of foreshadowing the result in this preliminary chapter. Yet there would be little excuse for another book about Carlyle if it were not fairly certain, at the outset, that we are dealing with a writer who perceived in an extraordinary way, the worth of the individual man, and who had an overwhelming sense of the infinite background of human life; and who therefore, in spite of his pessimism, became a seer and a prophet of idealism.

CHAPTER VII

HOW HE WROTE

CARLYLE'S marvellous faculty for expression was the result of mental qualities which made the facile prose composition of many professional writers impossible to him. He had to toil over each one of his tasks, as if he were writing a book for the first time, and almost as if he were writing for the first time in English. Like a Canadian wood-chopper, he grunted with each stroke of the ax; but if there was a grunt with every stroke, there was also a stroke for every grunt. His impatient or despairing exclamations give picturesqueness to his letters; his daily task on his *Cromwell* becomes, in the Carlylese vocabulary, "a real descent to Hades, to Golgotha and Chaos!" But he never stopped chopping for all that.

A few of his comments upon his *French Revolution,* as the work progressed, illuminate the truly artistic instinct of this toiler, who usually had only

40

words of scorn for "Art." Before attempting to portray the *Revolution* itself, he had tried his hand, it will be remembered, at *The Diamond Necklace,* in order "to prove myself in the narrative style." One would say to-day that the proof was tolerably clear! Yet he thought his own style, in this period, "far from the right;" *The Diamond Necklace* "is very far from pleasing me." He began writing *The French Revolution* in September, 1834, "with a kind of trembling hope," but after two weeks of labor he had produced but two pages of copy, and even these, "alas! not in the right style, not in the style that can stand." After a few months he reports that his book is proceeding "dreadfully slowly" but is "otherwise better than anything that I have done." The burning of the manuscript, through the carelessness of John Stuart Mill's maid, destroyed the result of five months' labor; but it was characteristic of the indomitable Scotchman that he straightway purchased a better quality of writing paper, and after a week's holiday, set himself to the task of making a better book. But the style still gave him "great uneasiness": it seemed to him full of affectation. He writes on nevertheless, "with the force of fire, above all with the speed of fire." "Nor do

I mean to *investigate* much more about it," he writes to his wife in 1836, "but to splash down what I know, in large masses of colours; that it may look like a smoke-and-flame conflagration in the distance, —which it is." How well this canny Scot knew what he was doing, after all! "It is a wild savage Book," he wrote to Sterling when it was finished; "born in blackness, whirlwind and sorrow." "One of the savagest written for several centuries," he said to his brother John; and then he added coolly and shrewdly, in his next letter: "It will stand a great deal of *beating;* the critics are welcome to lay on; there is a kind of *Orson* life in it which they will not kill." Pleasantest of all is his quiet sentence to his mother in September, 1837: "They make a great talk about the Book; which seems to have succeeded in a far higher degree than I had looked for."

Carlyle's attitude toward his task is equally clear in his comments upon the annotation of *Cromwell's Letters and Speeches.* Here are a few sentences from his correspondence with Emerson (the italics are Carlyle's) :

"I know no method of much consequence, except that of *believing,* of being *sincere;* from Homer and the Bible down to the poorest Burns's song, I find no other art which promises to be perennial.

"I grow daily to honor Facts more and more, and Theory less and less. A Fact, it seems to me, is a great thing: a Sentence printed if not by God, then at least by the Devil.

"I have often thought of Cromwell and Puritans; but do not see how the subject can be presented *still alive*. A subject dead is not worth presenting.

"I am now over head and ears in *Cromwellian* books; studying, for perhaps the fourth time in my life, to see if it be possible to get any creditable face-to-face acquaintance with our English Puritan period; or whether it must be left forever a mere hearsay and echo to one. Books equal in dulness were at no epoch of the world penned by unassisted man. Nevertheless, courage! I have got, within the last twelve months, actually as it were, to *see* that Cromwell was one of the greatest souls born of the English Kin; a great amorphous semi-articulate *Baresark;* very interesting to me. I grope in the dark vacuity of Baxters, Neales; thankful for here a glimpse, there a glimpse.

"I had begun to write some book on Cromwell. . . . There is risk yet, that with the loss of still farther labour, I may have to abandon it; and then the great dumb Oliver may lie unspoken forever; gathered to the mighty *Silent* of the earth; for, I think, there will hardly ever live another man that will believe in him and his Puritanism as I do. To *him* small matter.

"You ask after *Cromwell*: ask not of him; he is like to drive me mad. There he lies, shining *clear* enough to me, nay glowing, or painfully *burning;* but far down; sunk under the hundred years of Cant, Oblivion, Unbelief, and Triviality of every kind; through all which, and to the top of all which, what mortal industry or energy will avail to raise him! A thousand times I have rued that my poor activity ever took that direction. The likelihood still is that I may abandon the task undone. . . . There is no use of writing of things past, unless they can be made in fact things present."

In all these passages Carlyle emphasizes an intense vision of the Fact, and intense belief in it, as the cardinal laws of historical writing. Generally speaking, he had a contempt for all formal methods of literary composition. Froude quotes a characteristic utterance:

"Of Dramatic Art, though I have eagerly listened

to a Goethe speaking of it, and to several hundreds of others mumbling and trying to speak of it, I find that I, practically speaking, know yet almost as good as nothing. Indeed, of Art generally (*Kunst,* so called), I *can* almost know nothing. My first and last secret of *Kunst* is to get a thorough *intelligence* of the *fact* to be painted, represented, or, in what ever way, set forth—the *fact* deep as Hades, high as heaven, and written *so,* as to the visual face of it on our poor earth. This once blazing within me, if it will ever get to blaze, and bursting to be out, one has to take the whole dexterity of adaptation one is master of, and with tremendous struggling, contrive to exhibit it, one way or the other. This is not *Art*. I know well. It is Robinson Crusoe, and not the master of Woolwich, building a ship. Yet at bottom is there any Woolwich builder for such kinds of craft? What *Kunst* had Homer? What *Kunst* had Shakespeare? Patient, docile, valiant intelligence, conscious and unconscious, gathered from all winds, of these two things—their own faculty of utterance, and the audience they had to utter to, rude theater, Ithacan Farm Hall, or whatever it was—add only to which as the soul of the whole, the above-said blazing, radiant insight into the fact, blazing, burning interest about it, and we have the whole Art of Shakespeare and Homer."

It should be added that in the composition of *Cromwell,* and of *The French Revolution,* Carlyle was unable, through the very defects of his extraordinary qualities, to avail himself of conventional methods of note-taking; he had to carry his notes "in the living mind," however great might be the strain of the constantly focused attention. He wrote to the Reverend Alexander Scott in 1845:

"You ask me how I proceed in taking notes on such occasions. I would very gladly tell you all my methods if I had any; but really I have as it were none. I go into the business with all the intelligence, patience, silence, and other gifts and virtues that I have; find that ten or a hundred times as many could be profitably expended there, and still prove insufficient: and as for plan, I find that every new business requires as it were a new scheme of operations, which amid infinite bungling and plunging unfolds itself at intervals (very scantily after all) as I get along. The great thing is, Not to stop and break down; to know that virtue is very indispensable, that one must not stop because new and ever new drafts upon one's virtue must be honoured! But as to the special point of taking Excerpts, I think I universally, from habit or otherwise, rather avoid *writing* beyond the very minimum; mark in pencil the very smallest indication that will direct me to the thing again; and on the whole try to keep the whole matter simmering in the *living* mind and memory rather than laid up in paper bundles or otherwise laid up in the inert way. For this certainly turns out to be a truth: Only what you at last *have living* in your own memory and heart is worth putting down to be printed; this alone has much chance to get into the living heart and memory of other men. And here indeed, I believe, is the essence of all the rules I have ever been able to devise for myself. I have tried various schemes of arrangement and artificial helps to remembrance; paper-bags with labels, little paper-books, paper-bundles, etc., etc.; but the use of such things, I take it, depends on the habits and humours of the individual; what can be recommended universally seems to me mainly the above. My paper-bags (filled with little scraps all in pencil) have often enough come to little for me; and indeed in general when writing, I am surrounded with a rubbish of papers that have come to little :—this only will come to much for all of us,—To keep the thing you are elaborating as much as possible actually *in* your living mind; in order that this same mind, as much awake as possible, may have a chance to make something of it!—And so I will shut up my lumber shop again; and wish you right good speed in yours."

When this letter was written, Carlyle had already begun to read in preparation for his *Frederick the Great,* although many years were to pass before he actually began writing. Again we listen to the per-perpetual groanings that accompany his steady toil: he has no "sufficient love for lean Frederick and his heroisms"; he faces "by far the heaviest job ever laid upon me"; "I make no way in my Prussian history"; he has no "motive to go on, except the sad negative one, 'Shall we be beaten in our old days then?'" Of course he did make his way, in spite of impatience and disillusionment, and he was not beaten, because it was not in his nature to be beaten. But from his first book to his last, the inner struggle and the confessions of it remained much the same. There was always the agonizing effort to "see" the "fact," to penetrate to its real significance, to "believe" in its validity; and then to express the fact "sincerely," vividly, audibly,—as it were with the speaking voice.

In sheer visualizing power Carlyle surpassed any of his contemporaries, except possibly Dickens. Often of course, he had to set himself consciously to work to reconstruct a vanished scene. When, for instance, he visited the ancient battlefield of Dunbar in September, 1843, he wrote to his wife: "Having time to spare (for dinner was at six), I surveyed the old Castle, washed my feet in the sea, —smoking the while—took an image of Dunbar with me as I could, and then set my face to the wind and the storm." He "takes" the image, it will be observed, precisely as a photographer might "take" a picture, except that Carlyle is really looking at the swift confused masses of charging men, dead two hundred years before.

Another phrase, illuminating the dramatic, dynamic quality of Carlyle's visualization, occurs in his essay on Diderot: "As to this Diderot, had we once got so far that we could, in the faintest degree, personate him; take upon ourselves his character and his environment of circumstances, and act his Life over again, in that small Private Theater of ours (under our Hat),—*that* were what, in conformity with common speech, we should name *understanding* him, and could be abundantly content with."

The two passages just quoted are concerned with conscious professional effort to "see" the object imaginatively. But there are hundreds of pen-portraits in Carlyle's published works which seem to have resulted from the mere unconscious exposure of a highly sensitized retina: Carlyle sees and remembers and describes, as it were automatically.

"At the corner of Cockspur Street we paused for a moment, meeting Sir John Sinclair (Statistical Account of Scotland, etc.), whom I had never seen before and never saw again. A lean old man, tall but stooping, in tartan cloak, face very wrinkly, nose blue, physiognomy vague and with distinction as one might have expected it to be."

His single picture-making epithets are famous. "Lion" Mirabeau, "sea-green" Robespierre, "Grandison-Cromwell" Lafayette are familiar examples. But his nick-naming skill is matched by his ability to hit off a character with a volley of unexpected adjectives. "Jemmy Belcher was a smirking little dumpy Unitarian bookseller." "Coleridge, a puffy, anxious, obstructed-looking, fattish old man."

The student of Carlyle's craftsmanship can not spend a few days more profitably than in collecting for himself such examples of Carlyle's instantaneous photography. He should notice how the portraits etched with a line or two compare in technique and in effectiveness with the half-length and full-length figures which crowd the Carlyle gallery.

Here is Southey, described in a single sentence for the benefit of Emerson:

"Southey's complexion is still healthy mahogany-brown, with a fleece of white hair, and eyes that seem running at full gallop."

Three years earlier, in 1835, Carlyle had entered this fuller description of Southey in his diary:

"A lean, grey, whiteheaded man of dusky complexion, unexpectedly tall when he rises and still leaner then—the shallowest chin, prominent snubbed Roman nose, small carelined brow, huge bush of white grey hair on high crown and projecting on all sides, the most vehement pair of faint hazel eyes I have ever seen—a well-read, honest, limited (straight-laced even), kindly-hearted, most irritable man."

Thirty-two years later, Carlyle sketched Southey once more, in his *Reminiscences:*

"Southey was a man towards well up in the fifties;
hair grey, not yet hoary, well setting off his fine
clear brown complexion; head and face both small-
ish, as indeed the figure was while seated; features
finely cut; eyes, brow, mouth, good in their kind—
expressive all, even vehemently so, but betokening
rather keenness than depth either of intellect or
character; a serious, human, honest, but sharp, almost fierce-looking thin man, with very much of the
militant in his aspect,—in the eyes especially was
visible a mixture of sorrow and of anger, or of
angry contempt, as if his indignant fight with the
world had not yet ended in victory, but also never
should in defeat."

Here are two portraits of Alfred Tennyson,
drawn in the eighteen-forties:

"One of the finest-looking men in the world. A
great shock of rough dusty-dark hair; bright-laugh-
ing hazel eyes; massive aquiline face, most massive
yet most delicate; of sallow-brown complexion, almost Indian-looking; clothes cynically loose, free-
and-easy;—smokes infinite tobacco. His voice is
musical metallic,—fit for loud laughter and piercing
wail, and all that may lie between; speech and

speculation free and plenteous: I do not meet, in these late decades, such company over a pipe!—We shall see what he will grow to."

"A fine, large-featured, dim-eyed, bronze-coloured, shaggy-headed man is Alfred; dusty, smoky, free and easy, who swims outwardly and inwardly with great composure in an inarticulate element of tranquil chaos and tobacco smoke. Great now and then when he does emerge—a most restful, brotherly, solid-hearted man."

The picture of DeQuincey, in the *Reminiscences,* is unforgetable:

"He was a pretty little creature, full of wire-drawn ingenuities, bankrupt enthusiasms, bankrupt pride, with the finest silver-toned low voice, and most elaborate gently winding courtesies and ingenuities in conversation. 'What wouldn't one give to have him in a box, and take him out to talk!' That was Her criticism of him, and it was right good. A bright, ready, and melodious talker, but in the end an inclusive and long-winded. One of the smallest man figures I ever saw; shaped like a pair of tongs, and hardly above five feet in all. When he sate, you would have taken him, by candlelight,

for the beautifullest little child; blue-eyed, spark-
ling face, had there not been a something, too, which
said '*Eccovi*—this child has been in hell.'"

Here is another proof of Carlyle's possession of
the detective's eyesight and memory. In visiting the
Model Prison described in one of *The Latter-Day
Pamphlets* he recognized a man whom he had seen
once on the street a year before:

"From an upper room or gallery, we looked down
into a range of private courts, where certain Char-
tist Notabilities were undergoing their term. Char-
tist Notability First struck me very much; I had
seen him about a year before, by involuntary accident and much to my disgust, magnetizing a silly
young person; and had noted well the unlovely
voracious look of him, his thick oily skin, his heavy
dull-burning eyes, his greedy mouth, the dusky potent insatiable *animalism* that looked out of every
feature of him: a fellow adequate to animal-mag-
netize most things, I did suppose;—and here was
the post I now found him arrived at."

For a final example of Carlyle's descriptive power
let us turn from the world of men to the world of
apes, and read this parable from *Past and Present:*

"Perhaps few narratives in History or Mythology

are more significant than that Moslem one, of Moses
and the Dwellers by the Dead Sea. A tribe of men
dwelt on the shores of that same Asphaltic Lake;
and having forgotten, as we are all too prone to do,
the inner facts of Nature, and taken up with the
falsities and semblances of it, were fallen into sad
conditions,—verging indeed toward a certain far
deeper Lake. Whereupon it pleased kind Heaven
to send them the Prophet Moses, with an instructive
word of warning, out of which might have sprung
'remedial measures' not a few. But no: the men of
the Dead Sea discovered, as the valet-species always
does in heroes or prophets, no comeliness in Moses;
listened with real tedium to Moses, with light grinning, or with splenetic sniffs and sneers, affecting
even to yawn; and signified in short, that they
found him a humbug and even a bore. Such was
the candid theory these men of the Asphalt Lake
formed to themselves of Moses, That probably he
was a humbug, that certainly he was a bore.

"Moses withdrew; but Nature and her rigorous
veracities did not withdraw. The men of the Dead
Sea, when we next went to visit them, were all
'changed into Apes'; sitting on the trees there,
grinning now in the most *un*affected manner; gibber-

ing and chattering very genuine nonsense; finding
the whole Universe now a most indisputable Humbug. The Universe has *become* a Humbug to these
Apes who thought it one. There they sit and chatter, to this hour: only, I believe, every Sabbath
there returns to them a bewildered half-conscious-
ness, half-reminiscence; and they sit, with their
wizened smoke-dried visages, and such an air of
supreme tragicality as Apes may; looking out
through those blinking smoke-bleared eyes of theirs,
into the wonderfulest universal smoky Twilight and
undecipherable disordered Dusk of Things; wholly
an Uncertainty, Unintelligibility, they and it; and
for commentary thereon, here and there an unmusical chatter or mew:—truest, tragicalest Humbug
conceivable by the mind of man or ape! They made
no use of their souls; and so have lost them. Their
worship on the Sabbath now is to roost there, with
unmusical screeches, and half remember that they
had souls.

"Didst thou never, O Traveller, fall in with parties of this tribe? Meseems they are grown somewhat numerous in our day."

To print examples of Carlyle's manner of writing
is no doubt easier than to explain how he came to

write as he did. Yet certain extracts of his workmanship are plainly to be accounted for. The oral characteristics of his style, its exaggeration and its humor, are in part an inheritance and imitation of his father's talk in Annandale. Richter and other German romanticists encouraged him, no doubt, in a restless wilfulness, a dislike of the beaten paths. But his choice of words and sentence-structure, like his whole method of composition, was really necessitated by his physical organization. He exhibited, in an extraordinary degree, a combination of what are known as the "visual," the "audile" and the "motor" types of imagination. If his sensitiveness to visual impressions resembles that of Dickens, as we have said, in his nervous response to stimuli of sound he is like Walt Whitman, and in his motor type of imaginative energy he is another Tolstoi. Artists of this motor type think with their whole body. Their nerve centers compel them, whether they will or no, to a perpetual dynamic activity. They can not help creating a "Private Theater under their own Hat" and turning actors in it. They write in terms of bodily sensation.

An illustration may make this clearer. One of my pupils once marked four hundred and thirty-two passages in Carlyle's *French Revolution* as being "striking." When he was asked to analyse these passages and to discover, if possible, the reason for the impression they had made upon him, he found that nineteen per cent. of them—nearly one passage in every five—contained images of fire. Sixteen per cent. had images founded upon discordant noises, sixteen per cent., also, contained color terms, fifteen per cent. presented images of storm, wind and other violent physical changes in Nature, eleven per cent. had terms of confusion and chaos, and nearly eight per cent. were marked by metaphors drawn from the animal world. It may be added that thirty-five per cent. of the four hundred and thirty-two passages contained the "triad" construction—a three-fold grouping of words, clauses or sentences, familiar in the Bible and in many classical writers.

Of course it should be remembered that this particular pupil, in marking passages which appealed to him, betrayed, no doubt, something of his own type of physical organization and his own imaginative response to verbal imagery. It should also be borne in mind that Carlyle produced, especially in his letters and early essays, hundreds of pages which were not composed in the heightened "Carlylese" manner, and which are not easily to be distinguished, save by experts in English style, from other good writing of the Victorian period. Yet it remains true that he will continue to be judged as a writer by the passages which bear most intimately the mark of his temperament. At once a realist and a mystic, he was forced by the laws of his nature to see things in a certain way, and having perceived this vision, he had no rest in his soul or body until he had told what he had seen.

CHAPTER VIII

HIS LITERARY THEORY

CARLYLE'S method—instinctive and acquired —can be understood more easily if it is studied in connection with certain passages of his early critical essays, and with the theory of biography and history which he had evolved, long before he had attempted the great books which gave him fame.

It will be remembered that Carlyle began to study German in 1819, and that for a decade thereafter he busied himself chiefly with German literature. One of the results of his German studies was a quickening of his critical faculties, particularly in relation to the question of the nature of literature itself. In his *Life of Schiller,* his translations of German Romance, and above all in his translation of Goethe's *Wilhelm Meister,* the young Scotchman was compelled to grapple with some of the fundamental questions concerning poetry and prose.

60

His conception of the mood of the typical poet and of the function of genius was deeply influenced by Schiller. Though he came later, like so many other men, to discover that Goethe was greater than Schiller,—a "Bishop" in the diocese where Schiller remained merely a high-minded "Priest,"—Schiller's unconditional idealism became Carlyle's. In Richter he found "something splendid, wonderful, daring"; and his clear-cut portrayal of the singularities of Richter's style proves that Carlyle himself imitated Richter with his eyes wide open,—if he may fairly be said to have imitated him at all. Richter, said Carlyle, "in adopting his own extraordinary style, did it with clear knowledge of what excellence in style, and the various kinds and degrees of excellence therein, properly signified." In closing a remarkable essay on *The State of German Literature* Carlyle confesses that the spiritual aspect of Europe is melancholy, deserted of religious light: and yet he asserts that religion and poetry are eternal in the soul of man.

In the essay on Novalis he frankly adopts the philosophy and the terminology of Transcendentalism: to Novalis "Nature is no longer dead hostile Matter, but the veil and mysterious garment of the unseen." This doctrine was to become later the key-note of unforgetable passages in *Sartor Resartus*. Carlyle admits that Novalis was a Mystic, but he goes on to assert that "the Plummet of French or Scotch logic . . . will not sound the deep-seas of human Inquiry." Many a page was Carlyle destined to compose upon that theme!

But the notable essay on Goethe (*Foreign Review*, 1828), written four years after Carlyle's personal correspondence with the Olympian had begun, and four years before Goethe's death, affords the clearest demonstration of what Carlyle had learned from the master. Carlyle presents Goethe as "a clear and universal man." His "poetry is no separate faculty, no mental handicraft; but the voice of the whole harmonious manhood." There is embodied in Goethe "the Wisdom which is proper to this time; the beautiful, the religious Wisdom, which may still, with something of its old impressiveness, speak to the whole soul; still, in these hard, unbelieving days, reveal to us glimpses of the Unseen but not Unreal World, that so the Actual and the Ideal may again meet together, and clear Knowledge be again wedded to Religion, in the life and business of men." Goethe's poetry is thus "the poetry of our own day and generation. No demands are made on our credulity; the light, the science, the scepticism of our age, is not hid from us. . . . Poetry, as he views it, exists not in time or place, but in the spirit of man." The Poetry written by the Masters "aims not at 'furnishing a languid mind with fantastic shows and indolent emotions,' but at incorporating the everlasting Reason of man in forms visible to his Sense, and suitable to it."

This belief in the reality of Poetry, and in its high and enduring significance to man, was an essential article of Carlyle's literary creed. To produce literature worthy of the name one must conform to those conditions which are requisite for the production of poetry. One must possess a penetrating vision into facts and into those spiritual causes which lie back of facts; and one must be capable of that transforming imaginative power which incorporates the everlasting Reason into forms visible to the senses.

He gave a classic expression of this conviction in a passage of the lecture on *The Hero as Poet:*

"Nevertheless, you will say, there must be a difference between true Poetry and true Speech not poetical: what is the difference? On this point

many things have been written, especially by late
German Critics, some of which are not very intelligible at first. They say, for example, that the
Poet has an *infinitude* in him; communicates an
Unendlichkeit, a certain character of 'infinitude,'
to whatsoever he delineates. This, though not very
precise, yet on so vague a matter is worth remem-
bering: if well meditated, some meaning will gradually be found in it. For my own part, I find considerable meaning in the old vulgar distinction of
Poetry being *metrical,* having music in it, being a
song. Truly, if pressed to give a definition, one
might say this as soon as anything else: If your
delineation be authentically *musical,* musical not in
word only, but in heart and substance, in all thoughts
and utterances of it, in the whole conception of it,
then it will be poetical; if not, not.—Musical: how
much lies in that! A *musical* thought is one spoken
by a mind that has penetrated into the inmost heart
of the thing; detected the inmost mystery of it,
namely the *melody* that lies hidden in it; the inward
harmony of coherence which is its soul, whereby it
exists, and has a right to be, here in this world. All
inmost things, we may say, are melodious; naturally

utter themselves in Song. The meaning of Song goes deep. Who is there that, in logical words, can express the effect music has on us? A kind of inarticulate unfathomable speech, which leads us to the edge of the Infinite, and lets us for the moment gaze into that!

"Nay all speech, even the commonest speech, has something of the song in it: not a parish in the world but has its parish-accent;—the rythm or *tune* to which the people *sing* what they have to say! Accent is a kind of chanting; all men have accent of their own,—though they only *notice* that of others. Observe too how all passionate language does of itself become musical,—with a finer music than mere accent; the speech of a man in zealous anger becomes a chant, a song. All deep things are Song. It seems somehow the very central essence of us, Song; as if all the rest were but wrappings and hulls! The primal element of us; of us and of all things. The Greeks fabled of Sphere-Harmonies: it was the feeling they had of the inner structure of Nature; that the soul of all her voices and utterances was perfect music. Poetry, therefore, we will call *musical Thought*. The Poet is he who *thinks* in that manner. At bottom, it turns still on power of intellect; it is a man's sincerity and depth of vision that makes him a Poet. See deep enough, and you see musically; the heart of Nature *being* everywhere music, if you can only reach it."

As for the mere "art" of writing in verse, or for that matter in prose, Carlyle, as we have seen, troubled himself but little. If he could once see his facts "blazing," and was sure of their spiritual significance, the outward dress of words became to him a negligible detail. This was a dangerous laxity upon his part, no doubt; but his extraordinary native gift for expression made him reckless of all theories of style. But in his theory of the function of the imagination he is at one with most of the great creative artists who have tried to communicate in words their sense of the significant in art.

The particular form of literary art which Carlyle chose to follow led him straight to the fields of history and biography, and it happened that while he was writing some of his most memorable historical and biographical sketches, he also ventured to set forth his views as to the essential nature of the task which he had undertaken. A brief examination of his theory and practise, just before and after the *Sartor Resartus* period, will show the inner consistency of his method,—a method which may be traced in every one of his subsequent books.

CHAPTER IX

THE THEORY TESTED

LET us select, then, a half dozen essays written by Carlyle during the years immediately preceding and following the writing of *Sartor Resartus* in 1831. In these review articles, no one of which seems to have made a very profound impression at the moment, there will be found a summary of the working ideas which were soon to win for Carlyle his distinctive place in the world of letters.

Perhaps the best known essay of the group is the *Edinburgh Review* article on Burns (1828). Written ostensibly as a notice of Lockhart's *Life of Burns,* it passes without much delay to a fundamental discussion of the aim of Biography. Carlyle insists that if a man's life be written at all, "the public ought to be made acquainted with all the inward springs and relations of his character. How did coexisting circumstances modify him from without; how did he modify these from within? With

what endeavors and what efficacy rule over them;
with what resistance and what suffering sink under
them? In one word, what and how produced was
the effect of society on him; what and how produced was his effect on society? He who should
answer these questions, in regard to any individual,
would, as we believe, furnish a model of perfection
in Biography." He then proceeds to a sympathetic
sketch of a poet in a prosaic age. The excellence of
Burns lay in his *"Sincerity*, his indisputable air of
Truth." He *sees* his object. His love and his indignation are genuine. The *Jolly Beggars* is thus
the most strictly poetical of Burns's "poems;" it is
"complete, a real self-supporting Whole;" but the
same wholeness, and an even truer inspiration is to
be found in his *Songs.* Burns failed, it is true, in
two indisputable matters: he had no Religion, and
he had no singleness of aim. Yet the world is
habitually unjust in its judgments of such men as
Burns and Byron. "Granted the ship comes into
harbor with shrouds and tackle damaged; the pilot
is blameworthy; he has not been all-wise and all-
powerful: but to know *how* blameworthy, tell us
first whether his voyage has been round the Globe,
or only to Ramsgate and the Isle of Dogs."

The sternness and tenderness and rich eloquence of this essay make it the most familiar example of what is sometimes termed Carlyle's "first manner." It is written in conformity with the best English eighteenth century style, only with more freedom and warmth and depth of coloring. Yet its importance is not as a pattern of writing, but in its typical Carlylese attitude toward the deep problems of life and literature.

The essay on *History* (1830) shows the same intimate sense of the difficulties in reaching an adequate judgment upon either the individual or the collective life. "Let any one who has examined the current of human affairs, and how intricate, perplexed, unfathomable, even when seen into with our own eyes, are their thousand-fold blending movements, say whether the true representing of it is easy or impossible. Social Life is the aggregate of all the individual men's Lives who constitute society; History is the essence of innumerable Biographies. But if one Biography, nay our own Biography, study and recapitulate it as we may, remains in so many points unintelligible to us; how much more must these million, the very facts of which, to say nothing of the purport of them, we know not, and can not know!"

How rare, Carlyle goes on to argue, is the faculty of insight into passing things! How much has been "passed over unnoticed, because no Seer, but only mere Onlookers, chanced to be there!" It is only the Seers who have a chance to become the true Artists in History, as distinguished from the artizans and mere recorders.

In the essay on *Biography* (*Fraser's Magazine,* April, 1832) Carlyle uses again his axiom: "History is the essence of innumerable Biographies." Biography combines poetic and scientific interest. Imaginative picture, for instance, is essentially biographic; and for all true biographic writing there is needed a Poet,—that is to say, not a verse-writer, but a man who can perceive and set forth the inexhaustible meanings of Reality. Here we reach the central point of Carlyle's theory: according to him all Reality, every Fact, is full of these inexhaustible meanings, waiting to be interpreted. Hence the infinite worth of Truth, the omnipotence of Belief. If Truth and Belief are there, how impressive becomes the smallest historical fact! And then come the marvellous pages in which Carlyle illustrates his creed:

". . . We ourselves can remember reading, in *Lord Clarendon,* with feelings perhaps somehow accidentally opened to it,—certainly with a depth of impression strange to us then and now,—that insignificant-looking passage, where Charles, after the battle of Worcester, glides down, with Squire Careless, from the Royal Oak, at nightfall, being hungry: how, 'making a shift to get over hedges and ditches, after walking at least eight or nine miles, which were the more grievous to the King by the weight of his boots (for he could not put *them* off when he cut off his hair, for want of shoes), before morning they came to *a poor cottage, the owner whereof, being a Roman Catholic, was known to Careless.'* How this poor drudge, being knocked up from his snoring, 'carried them into a little barn full of hay, which was a better lodging than he had for himself'; and by and by, not without difficulty, brought his Majesty 'a piece of bread and a great pot of buttermilk,' saying candidly that 'he himself lived by his daily labor, and that what he had brought him was the fare he and his wife had': on which nourishing diet his Majesty, 'staying upon the hay-mow,' feeds

thankfully for two days; and then departs, under
new guidance, having first changed clothes, down to
the very shirt and 'old pair of shoes,' with his land-
lord; and so, as worthy Bunyan has it, 'goes on his
way and sees him no more.' Singular enough, if
we will think of it! This, then, was a genuine
flesh-and-blood Rustic of the year 1651: he did actually swallow bread and buttermilk (not having
ale and bacon), and do field-labor: with these hob-
nailed 'shoes' has sprawled through mud-roads in
winter, and, jocund or not, driven his team a-field in
summer: he made bargains; had chafferings and
higglings, now a sore heart, now a glad one; was
born; was a son; was a father; toiled in many ways,
being forced to it, till the strength was all worn out
of him; and then—lay down 'to rest his galled back,'
and sleep there till the long-distant morning! How
comes it, that he alone of all the British rustics who
tilled and lived along with him, on whom the blessed
sun on that same 'fifth day of September' was
shining, should have chanced to rise on us; that this
poor pair of clouted Shoes, out of the million million hides that have been tanned, and cut, and worn,
should still subsist, and hang visibly together? We
see him but for a moment; for one moment, the

blanket of the Night is rent asunder, so that we behold and see, and then closes over him—forever.

"So too, in some *Boswell's Life of Johnson,* how indelible and magically bright does many a little *Reality* dwell in our remembrance! There is no need that the personages on the scene be a King and Clown; that the scene be the Forest of the Royal Oak, 'on the borders of Staffordshire': need only that the scene lie on this old firm Earth of ours, where we also have so surprisingly arrived; that the personages be *men,* and *seen* with the eyes of a man. Foolish enough, how some slight, perhaps mean and even ugly incident, if *real* and well presented, will fix itself in a susceptive memory, and lie ennobled there; silvered over with the pale cast of thought, with the pathos which belongs only to the Dead. For the Past is all holy to us; the Dead are all holy, even they that were base and wicked when alive. Their baseness and wickedness was not *They,* was but the heavy and unmanageable Environment that lay round them, with which they fought unprevailing: *they* (the ethereal god-given Force that dwelt in them, and was their *Self*) have now shuffled off that heavy Environment, and are free and pure: their lifelong Battle, go how it might, is all ended, with

many wounds or with fewer; they have been recalled from it, and the once harsh-jarring battlefield
has become a silent awe-inspiring Golgotha, and
Gottesacker (Field of God)!—Boswell relates this
in itself smallest and poorest of occurrences: 'As we
walked along the Strand to-night, arm in arm, a
woman of the town accosted us in the usual enticing
manner. 'No, no, my girl,' said Johnson; 'it won't
do.' He, however, did not treat her with harshness;
and we talked of the wretched life of such women.'
Strange power of *Reality!* Not even this poorest
of occurrences, but now, after seventy years are
come and gone, has a meaning for us. Do but consider that it is *true;* that it did in very deed occur!
That unhappy Outcast, with all her sins and woes,
her lawless desires, too complex mischances, her
wailings and her riotings, has departed utterly; alas!
her siren finery has got all besmutched, ground,
generations since, into dust and smoke; of her de-
graded body, and whole miserable earthly existence,
all is away: *she* is no longer here, but far from us,
in the bosom of Eternity,—whence we too came,
whither we too are bound! Johnson said, 'No, no,
my girl; it won't do'; and then 'we talked';—and
herewith the wretched one, seen but for the twink-

ling of an eye, passes on into the utter Darkness. No high Calista, that ever issued from story-teller's brain, will impress us more deeply than this meanest of the mean; and for a good reason: That *she* issued from the Maker of Men.

"It is well worth the Artist's while to examine for himself what it is that gives such pitiful incidents their memorableness; his aim likewise is, above all things, to be *memorable*. Half the effect, we already perceive, depends on the object; on its being *real,* on its being really *seen*. The other half will depend on the observer, and the question now is: How are real objects to be *so* seen, on what quality of observing, or of style in describing, does this so intense pictorial power depend? Often a slight circumstance contributes curiously to the result—some little, and perhaps to appearance accidental, feature is presented; a light-gleam, which instantaneously *excites* the mind, and urges it to complete the picture and evolve the meaning thereof for itself. By critics, such light-gleams and their almost magical influence have frequently been noted: but the power to produce such, to select such features as will produce them, is generally treated as a knack, or trick of the trade, a secret for being 'graphic'; whereas these magical feats are, in truth, rather inspirations; and the gift of performing them, which acts unconsciously, without forethought, and as if by nature alone, is properly a *genius* for description.

"One grand, invaluable secret there is, however, which includes all the rest, and, what is comfortable, lies clearly in every man's power: *To have an open, loving heart, and what follows from the possession of such.* Truly it has been said, emphatically in these days ought it to be repeated, A loving Heart is the beginning of all Knowledge. This it is that opens the whole mind, quickens every faculty of the intellect to do its fit work, that of *knowing;* and therefrom, by sure consequence, of vividly *uttering-forth.* Other secret for being 'graphic' is there none, worth having: but this is an all-sufficient one. See, for example, what a small Boswell can do! Hereby, indeed, is the whole man made a living mirror, wherein the wonders of this ever-wonderful Universe are, in their true light (which is ever a magical, miraculous one) represented, and reflected back on us. It has been said, 'the heart sees farther than the head'; but, indeed, without the seeing heart, there is no true seeing for the head so much as possible; all is mere *oversight,* hallucination and vain superficial phantasmagoria, which can permanently profit no one.

"Here, too, may we not pause for an instant and make a practical reflection? Considering the multitude of mortals that handle the Pen in these days, and can mostly spell and write without glaring violations of grammar, the question naturally arises: How is it, then, that no Work proceeds from them, bearing any stamp of authenticity and permanence; of worth for more than one day? Shiploads of Fashionable Novels, Sentimental Rhymes, Tragedies, Farces, Diaries of Travel, Tales by flood and field, are swallowed monthly into the bottomless Pool. Still does the Press toil: innumerable Papermakers, Compositors, Printers' Devils, Bookbinders and Hawkers grown hoarse with loud proclaiming, rest not from their labour: and still, in torrents, rushes on the great array of Publications, unpausing, to their final home; and still Oblivion, like the Grave, cries, Give! give! How is it that of all these countless multitudes, no one can attain to the smallest mark of excellence, or produce aught that shall endure longer than 'snow-flake on the river' or the foam of penny beer? We answer: Because they *are* foam; because there is no *Reality* in them. These

three thousand men, women and children that make up the army of British Authors do not, if we will consider it, *see* anything whatever, consequently *have* nothing that they can record and utter, only more or fewer things that they can plausibly pretend to record. The Universe, of Man and Nature, is still quite shut up from them, the 'open secret' still utterly a secret; because no sympathy with Man or Nature, no love and free simplicity of heart has yet unfolded the same. Nothing but a pitiful Image of their own pitiful Self, with its vanities and grudgings and ravenous hunger of all kinds, hangs forever painted in the retina of these unfortunate persons; so that the starry All, with whatsoever it embraces, does not appear as some expanded magic-lantern shadow of that same Image,—and naturally looks pitiful enough.

"It is vain for these persons to allege that they are naturally without gift, naturally stupid and sightless, and so *can* attain to no knowledge of anything; therefore, in writing of anything, must need write falsehoods of it, there being in it no truth for them. Not so, good friends. The stupidest of you has a certain faculty; were it but that of articulate speech (say, in the Scottish, the Irish, the Cockney dialect, or even in 'Governess-English'), and of physically discerning what lies under your nose. The stupidest of you would perhaps grudge to be compared in faculty with James Boswell; yet see what he has produced! You do not use your faculty honestly; your heart is shut up; full of greediness, malice, discontent; so your intellectual sense can not be open. It is vain also to urge that James Boswell had opportunities; saw great men and great things, such as you can never hope to look on. What make ye of Parson White in Selborne? He had not only no great men to look on, but not even men; merely sparrows and cock-chafers: yet he has left us a *Biography* of these; which, under its title, *Natural History of Selborne*, still remains valuable to us, which has copied a little sentence or two *faithfully* from the Inspired Volume of Nature, and so is itself not without inspiration. Go ye and do likewise. Sweep away utterly all frothiness and falsehood from your heart; struggle unweariedly to acquire, what is possible for every God-created man, a free, open, humble soul; *speak not at all, in any wise, till you have somewhat to speak;* care not for the *reward* of your speaking; but simply and with undivided mind for the *truth* of your speaking: then be placed in what section of Space and of Time soever, do but open your eyes, and they shall actually *see,* and bring you real *knowledge,* wondrous, worthy of *belief;* and instead of one Boswell and one White, the world will rejoice in a thousand, stationed on their thousand several watch-towers,— to instruct us by indubitable documents, of whatsoever in our so stupendous World comes to light and *is!* Oh, had the Editor of this Magazine but a magic rod to turn all that not inconsiderable Intellect, which now deluges us with artificial fictitious soap-lather and mere Lying, into the faithful study of *Reality,*—what knowledge of great, everlasting Nature, and of Man's ways and doings therein, would not every year bring us in! Can we but change one single soap-latherer and mountebank Juggler, into a true Thinker and Doer, who even *tries* honestly to think and do,—great will be our reward."

No passage that Carlyle ever wrote deserves closer study, for it sets forth not only his theory as to the writing of History and Biography, and his underlying philosophy of Reality, but also the personal qualities which he deemed essential to the performance of the work which was to fill the remainder of his life.

The closing paragraphs of the essay on Biography are devoted to Boswell's *Life of Johnson,* which had been re-edited by Croker in 1831. Carlyle promises an extended review of the five volumes in the following number of *Fraser's Magazine* (May, 1832). This essay, which is probably more familiar to the general reader than any of Carlyle's essays except the *Burns,* is devoted to a concrete demonstration of the theoretical principle laid down in the essay on Biography. Boswell, it appears, had the "open, loving heart," the spirit of discipleship and of hero-worship. And this was the secret of his insight: "The heart sees further than the head." This book, therefore, was True, and possessing Reality, it was for that reason genuine Poetry. In the pages of Boswell men can still see the immortal figure of "great-souled Samuel," the "prophet of the English," the "last genuine Tory." Johnson was a "Brave Man," endowed with the talent of Silence; a lover of Truth, a hater of Cant. "His Doings and Writings are not *shows* but *performances*: you may weigh them in the balance, and they will stand

weight."   And Mercy dwells with Johnson's Valor;
"a true brother of men is he; and filial lover of the
Earth."   He had of course his prejudices, his blindness to the European movement of ideas.   But, as
Browning was to say long afterward,

> "So we half-men struggle."

Could we but combine,—Carlyle declares in closing,—the Candor and Clearness of Hume with the
Reverence, the Love and devout Humility of Johnson, we should have "the whole man of a new time."

"The whole man of a new time": those words
are a sort of pivot on which the Carlyle theory of
history and biography swings into the Carlyle
theory of conduct.   Endowed with a strong ethical
sense and an acute social consciousness, it was as
natural for this man as it was for Count Tolstoi
to ask "What then is to be *done?*"   In *Sartor*, in
Heroes, in *Chartism* and in *The Latter-Day Pamphlets* we shall see this vision of the "new time,"—
the epoch chanted by Tennyson in his first *Locks-
ley Hall,* and described in the novels of Charles
Dickens.   All of Carlyle's books, in fact, might be
characterized as "Tracts for the Times."   The end
of life is not Thought, but Action; this is the key

in which the motor-minded Scotchman was to write for thirty years.

In the revelatory group of essays which we are now reviewing, the clearest confession of Carlyle's theory of conduct will be found in *Signs of the Times* (1829) and *Characteristics* (1831). The first of these essays preceded the composition of *Sartor,* and the second was Carlyle's first piece of writing after *Sartor* was finished. Taken together, they contain almost every article of Carlyle's ethical and social creed.

He begins *Signs of the Times,* for example, by declaring that "Our grand business undoubtedly is not to *see* what lies dimly at a distance, but to *do* what lies clearly at hand." The Age of Machinery in which men are living has led to a loss of faith in individual endeavor. It is not merely Science and Philosophy that are conducted on mechanical principles, the same faith in mere mechanism is visible in Politics. But since human love and fear are infinite, no finite mechanism can be a source of happiness. Profit and loss are not final agents. "Dynamic" as well as "mechanical" forces are needed for the true conduct of life. Faith counts for more than "logic." "One man that has a higher Wisdom, a hitherto unknown spiritual truth in him, is stronger, not than ten men that have it not, or than ten thousand, but than *all* men that have it not." And Carlyle closes by asserting his "faith in the imperishable dignity of man." The world is still "plastic, infinite, divine." Though the time is sick and out of joint, and the thinking minds of all nations call for change, there is nevertheless hope for humanity under a higher guidance than ours. The only solid reformation is what each man "begins and perfects on himself."

Characteristics—a title borrowed from the famous essay of Fichte—is even more rich than *Signs of the Times* in those pregnant thoughts and phrases which were destined to become the burden of Carlyle's teaching to his generation. Nowhere has he explained more suggestively that doctrine of "Silence" which has often been misunderstood even by Carlyle's followers. Let us see how he develops it. The test of the right working of all vital powers, he asserts, is unconsciousness. Unity is always silent; it is discord that is loud. Unconsciousness is the sign of health. "Of our thinking, we might say, it is but the mere upper surface that we shape into articulate thoughts;—underneath the region of

argument and conscious discourse, lies the region of
meditation; here, in its quiet mysterious depths,
dwells what vital force is in us; here, if aught is to
be created, and not merely manufactured and com-
municated, must the work go on." (*"Elan vital,"*
as Bergson might say!) Hence the distinction,
touched upon in an earlier essay, between the "man
of logic" and the "man of insight." But this distinction is equally true of conduct, and of the life of
society. The Body Politic must be Unconscious, if
it is to perform its functions rightly. This unconscious performance of function is "Silence," "Harmony," "Life" itself. But our actual contemporary
society, says Carlyle, is intensely self-conscious, or,
in other words, diseased. "Man remains unserved,
he has subdued this Planet, his habitation and inheritance; yet reaps no profit from the victory.
. . . Countries are rich, prosperous in all manner of increase, beyond example: but the *Men*
of those countries are poor, needier than ever of all
sustenance outward and inward; of Belief, of
Money, of Food."

It will be noticed that Carlyle, the child of Calvinism, puts "Belief" first in this list of wants. He
finds that vitality has fled from religion: with self-

consciousness it has become less potent and more mechanical. Inspiration is disappearing from literature. And the remedy, if there be a remedy for these social ills? It lies in the Aristotelian maxim: "The end of man is an Action, not a Thought." We are to be saved through Work, and there can be no creative labor without Faith. New captains of men must be sought after, and they must govern by loyalty. "The Age of Miracles, as it ever was, *now is*"; the deep, vital, unconscious forces of the world beat through the pulses of every man who labors in faith. Whatsoever, then, thy hand findeth to do, do it with thy might.

Carlyle never wrote with more moving power, and rarely did he write, in his later days, with such assurance of social faith. He had just worked out, in *Sartor,* the problem of the individual; and now, as we re-read *Characteristics,* we can trace the high-water mark of his hopes for the communal life. For undeniably, these hopes were fated to ebb. Carlyle thundered and lightened in book after book his magnificent antiphonals of Silence and Labor and Loyalty; but his new Captains of humanity not being discoverable—by him—he gradually lost faith in the progress of society, and after glorifying

Cromwell and Mahomet and Mirabeau he ended by chanting the praises of the "beneficent whip" and of lean Frederick of Prussia.

We must turn now to this series of famous books, and note in them the reappearance and the modification of those fundamental thoughts and those instinctive modes of workmanship which we have just been observing in the Essays.

CHAPTER X

SARTOR RESARTUS

SARTOR RESARTUS ("The Tailor Patched") is, as Garnett has said, a "book spun from a single metaphor." It professes to deal with the Philosophy of Clothes: the inner meaning is that man and society are only vestures,—transient wrappings and symbols of the one Reality, God. Carlyle found the framework of his idea in Swift's *Tale of a Tub.* At first, he played with this notion of Vestures (—"I am going to write—Nonsense") intending a mere magazine article, but the thought took possession of him, and he wrote on impetuously during the first six months of 1831 until, as Professor MacMechan says in his admirable edition of *Sartor,* he had drawn "into the compass of a single volume all the best that he had thought in his past life."

In outward form, the book is a literary hoax. It claims to be an account by an "English editor" of a singular book on "Clothes, their Origin and Influence" (*"Die Kleider, ihr Werden und Wirken"*) which had just been published in Germany. The author was a certain Diogenes Teufelsdröckh ("God-Born Devil's-Dung"), Professor of Things in General at the University of Weiss-nicht-wo, that is to say "Nowhere,"—"Utopia." The Professor's book, which the "editor" can present only in fragments, is in three parts. The first and third are devoted to various aspects of clothes-philosophy, but the second professes to be an autobiography of Teufelsdröckh himself. Carlyle utilizes this second part to tell the epoch-making phases of his own development, from earliest childhood. The imaginary German village of Entepfuhl ("Duck-pond") is really Ecclefechan; "Hinterschlag" Academy is Annan, and the "nameless" University is Edinburgh. But this actual autobiography of Carlyle is mingled throughout with pure fantasy, with passages from Carlyle's abortive romance *Wotton Reinfred,* and with grave circumstantial descriptions of German life, in the manner of Defoe and Swift. *Sartor,* therefore, conforms to Dryden's definition of Satire in that it is "full of various matter"; and it also takes the full liberty of Satire in its range of

style. Inventing a "German" book for the English
public of the eighteen-thirties,—whose sole notion
of things "German" was that they were likely to be
queer,—Carlyle gave full rein to his talent for fool-
ery and for grotesque extravagance. At bottom,
as in all his books, there is a perfectly clear and simple plan, evolved by a cunning literary artist, but
the surface of *Sartor* is ruffled and blown this way
and that by the whimsical, bedevilling humors of a
master satirist.

We must limit ourselves to five passages from
Sartor. Each is very famous and needs little or no
elucidation. The first is the description (Book I,
Chapter 3) of Teufelsdröckh's watch-tower, in the
city of Weissnichtwo.

The Watch-Tower

"To the Editor of these sheets, as to a young en-
thusiastic Englishman, however unworthy, Teufelsdröckh opened himself perhaps more than to the
most. Pity only that we could not then half guess
his importance, and scrutinise him with due power
of vision! We enjoyed, what not three men in
Weissnichtwo could boast of, a certain degree of
access to the Professor's private domicile. It was the

attic floor of the highest house in the Wahngasse;
and might truly be called the pinnacle of Weissnichtwo, for it rose sheer up above the contiguous
roofs, themselves rising from elevated ground.
Moreover, with its windows, it looked towards all
the four *Orte,* or as the Scotch say, and we ought to
say, *Airts:* the Sitting-room itself commanded
three; another came to view in the *Schlafgemach*
(Bed-room) at the opposite end; to say nothing of
the Kitchen, which offered two, as it were *duplicates,*
and showing nothing new. So that it was in fact
the speculum or watch-tower of Teufelsdröckh;
wherefrom, sitting at ease, he might see the whole
life-circulation of that considerable City; the streets
and lanes of which, with all their doing and driving
(*Thun und Treiben*), were for the most part visible
there.

" 'I look down into all that wasp-nest or bee-hive,'
have we heard him say, 'and witness their wax-lay-
ing and honey-making, and poison-brewing, and
choking by sulphur. From the Palace esplanade,
where music plays while Serene Highness is pleased
to eat his victuals, down to the low lane, where in
her door-sill the aged widow, knitting for a thin live-
lihood, sits to feel the afternoon sun, I see it all; for,

except the Schlosskirche weathercock, no biped stands so high. Couriers arrive bestrapped and be-booted, bearing Joy and Sorrow bagged-up in pouches of leather; there, topladen, and with four swift horses, rolls-in the country Baron and his household; here, on timber-leg, the lamed Soldier hops painfully along, begging alms : a thousand car-riages, and wains, and cars, come tumbling-in with Food, with young Rusticity, and other Raw Pro-duce, inanimate or animate, and go tumbling out again with Produce manufactured. That living flood, pouring through these streets, of all quali-ties and ages, knowest thou whence it is coming, whither it is going? *Aus der Ewigkeit, zu der Ewig-keit hin:* From Eternity, onward to Eternity! These are Apparitions: what else? Are they not souls rendered visible; in Bodies, that took shape and will lose it, melting into air? Their solid pavement is a Picture of the Sense; they walk on the bosom of Nothing, blank Time is behind them and before them. Or fanciest thou, the red and yellow Clothes-screen yonder, with spurs on its heels, and feather in its crown, is but of Today, without a Yesterday or a Tomorrow; and had not rather its Ancestor alive when Hengst and Horsa overran thy Island?

Friend, thou seest here a living link in that Tissue of History, which inweaves all Being: watch well, or it will be past thee, and seen no more.

" '*Ach, mein Lieber!*' said he once, at midnight, when he had returned from the Coffee-house in rather earnest talk, 'it is a true sublimity to dwell here. These fringes of lamp-light, struggling up through smoke and thousandfold exhalation, some fathoms into the ancient reign of Night, what thinks Boötes of them, as he leads his Hunting-Dogs over the Zenith, in their leash of sidereal fire? That stifled hum of Midnight, when Traffic has lain down to rest; and the chariot-wheels of Vanity, still rolling here and there through distant streets, are bearing her to Halls roofed-in, and lighted to the due pitch for her; and only Vice and Misery, to prowl or to moan like nightbirds, are abroad; that hum I say, like the stertorous, unquiet slumber of sick Life; is heard in Heaven! Oh, under that hideous coverlet of vapors, and putrefactions, and unimaginable gases, what a Fermenting-vat lies simmering and hid! The joyful and the sorrowful are there; men are dying there, men are being born, men are praying,—on the other side of a brick partition, men

are cursing; and around them all is the vast, void
Night. The proud Grandee still lingers in his per-
fumed saloons, or reposes within damask curtains;
Wretchedness cowers into truckle-beds, or shivers
hunger-stricken into its lair of straw: in obscure
cellars, *Rouge-et-Noir* languidly emits its voice-of-
destiny to haggard hungry Villains; while Councillors of State sit plotting, and playing their high
chess-game, whereof the pawns are Men. The
Lover whispers his mistress that the coach is ready;
and she, full of hope and fear, glides down, to fly
with him over the borders: the Thief, still more silently, sets-to his picklocks and crowbars, or lurks
in wait till the watchmen first snore in their boxes.
Gay mansions, with supper-rooms, and dancing-
rooms, are full of light and music and high-swelling
hearts; but, in the Condemned Cells, the pulse of
life beats tremulous and faint, and bloodshot eyes
look out through the darkness, which is around and
within, for the light of a stern last morning. Six
men are to be hanged on the morrow: comes no
hammering from the *Rabenstein?*—their gallows
must even now be o' building. Upwards of five-hun-
dred-thousand two-legged animals without feathers

lie around us, in horizontal positions; their heads all in nightcaps, and full of the foolishest dreams. Riot cries aloud, and staggers and swaggers in his rank dens of shame; and the Mother, with streaming hair, kneels over her pallid dying infant, whose cracked lips only her tears now moisten.—All these heaped and huddled together, with nothing but a little carpentry and masonry between them;— crammed in, like salted fish, in their barrel; or weltering, shall I say, like an Egyptian pitcher of tamed Vipers, each struggling to get its *head above* the others: *such* work goes on under that smoke-counterpane!—But I, *mein Werther,* sit above it all; I am alone with the Stars.'

"We looked in his face to see whether, in the utterance of such extraordinary Night-thoughts, no feeling might be traced there; but with the light we had, which indeed was only a single tallow-light, and far enough from the window, nothing save that old calmness and fixedness was visible."

The second must be the well-known parable of Carlyle's own moment of revolt and illumination on Leith Walk, Edinburgh, in the summer of 1821 or 1822. (Book 2, Chapter 7.)

The Everlasting No

" 'So had it lasted,' concludes the Wanderer, 'so had it lasted, as in bitter protracted Death-agony, through long years. The heart within me, unvisited by any heavenly dewdrop, was smouldering in sulphurous, slow-consuming fire. Almost since earliest memory I had shed no tear; or one only when I, murmuring half-audibly, recited Faust's Deathsong, that wild *Selig der den er im Siegesglanze findet* (Happy whom *he* finds in Battle's splendour), and thought that of this last Friend even I was not forsaken, that Destiny itself could not doom me not to die. Having no hope, neither had I any definite fear, were it of Man or of Devil: nay, I often felt as if it might be solacing, could the Arch-Devil himself, though in Tartarean terrors, but rise to me, that I might tell him a little of my mind. And yet, strangely enough, I lived in a continual, indefinite, pining fear; tremulous, pusillanimous, apprehensive of I knew not what: it seemed as if all things in the Heavens above and the Earth beneath would hurt me; as if the Heavens and the Earth were but boundless jaws of a devouring monster wherein I, palpitating, waited to be devoured.

" 'Full of such humour, and perhaps the miserablest man in the whole French Capital or Suburbs, was I, one sultry Dog-day, after much perambulation, toiling along the dirty little *Rue Saint-Thomas de l'Enfer*, among civic rubbish enough, in a close atmosphere, and over pavements hot as Nebuchadnezzar's Furnace; whereby doubtless my spirits were little cheered; when all at once, there rose a Thought in me, and I asked myself: 'What *art* thou afraid of? Wherefore, like a coward, dost thou for ever pip and whimper, and go cowering and trembling? Despicable biped! what is the sum-total of the worst that lies before thee? Death? Well, Death; and say the pangs of Tophet too, and all that the Devil and Man may, will, or can do against thee! Hast thou not a heart; canst thou not suffer whatsoever it be; and, as a Child of Freedom, though outcast, trample Tophet itself under thy feet, while it consumes thee? Let it come, then; I will meet it and defy it!' And as I so thought, there rushed like a stream of fire over my whole soul; and I shook base Fear away from me forever. I was strong, of unknown strength; a spirit, almost a god. Ever from that time, the temper of my misery was changed: not

Fear or whining Sorrow was it, but Indignation and grim fire-eyed Defiance.

" 'Thus had the EVERLASTING No (*das ewige Nein*) pealed authoritatively through all the recesses of my Being, of my ME; and then was it that my whole ME stood up, in native God-created majesty, and with emphasis recorded its Protest. Such a Protest, the most important transaction in Life, may that same Indignation and Defiance, in a psychological point of view, be fitly called. The Everlasting No had said: 'Behold, thou art fatherless, outcast, and the Universe is mine (the Devil's);' to which my whole ME now made answer: '*I* am not thine, but Free, and forever hate thee!'

" 'It is from this hour that I incline to date my Spiritual New-birth, or Baphometic Fire-baptism; perhaps I directly thereupon began to be a Man.' "

The picture of War (Book 2, Chapter 7) is as ghastly true for the battle-summer of 1915 as it was for the campaigns of Napoleon.

War

" 'Horrible enough! A whole Marchfeld strewed with shell-splinters, cannon-shot, ruined tumbrils,

and dead men and horses; stragglers still remaining
not so much as buried. And those red mould heaps:
ay, there lie the Shells of Men, out of which all the
Life and Virtue has been blown; and now they are
swept together, and crammed-down out of sight, like
blown Egg-shells!—Did Nature, when she bade the
Donau bring down his mould-cargoes from the Ca-
rinthian and Carpathian Heights, and spread them
out here into the softest, richest level,—intend thee,
O Marchfeld, for a corn-bearing Nursery, whereon
her children might be nursed; or for a Cockpit,
wherein they might the more commodiously be throt-
tled and tattered? Were thy three broad highways,
meeting here from the ends of Europe, made for
Ammunition-wagons, then? Were thy Wagrams
and Stillfrieds but so many ready-built Casemates,
wherein the house of Hapsburg might batter with
artillery, and with artillery be battered? König
Ottokar, amid yonder hillocks, dies under Rodolf's
truncheon; here Kaiser Franz falls a-swoon under
Napoleon's: within which five centuries, to omit the
others, how hast thy breast, fair Plain, been defaced
and defiled! The greensward is torn-up and tram-
pled-down; man's fond care of it, his fruit-trees,
hedge-rows, and pleasant dwellings, blown-away

with gunpowder; and the kind seedfield lies a desolate, hideous Place of Sculls.——Nevertheless, Nature is at work; neither shall these Powder-Devilkins with their utmost devilry gainsay her: but all that gore and carnage will be shrouded-in, absorbed into manure; and next year the Marchfeld will be green, nay greener. Thrifty unwearied Nature, ever out of our great waste educing some little profit of thy own,——how dost thou, from the very carcass of the Killer, bring Life for the Living!

" 'What, speaking in quite unofficial language, is the net-purport and upshot of war? To my own knowledge, for example, there dwell and toil, in the British village of Dumdrudge, usually some five hundred souls. From these, by certain 'Natural Enemies' of the French, there are successively selected, during the French war, say thirty able-bodied men: Dumdrudge, at her own expense, has suckled and nursed them; she has, not without difficulty and sorrow, fed them up to manhood, and even trained them to crafts, so that one can weave, another build, another hammer, and the weakest can stand under thirty stone avoirdupois. Nevertheless, amid much weeping and swearing, they are selected; all dressed in red; and shipped away, at the public charges, some two-thousand miles, or say only to the south of Spain; and fed there till wanted. And now to that same spot in the south of Spain, are thirty similar French artisans, from a French Dumdrudge, in like manner wending: till at length, after infinite effort, the two parties come into actual juxtaposition; and Thirty stands fronting Thirty, each with a gun in his hand. Straightway the word 'Fire!' is given: and they blow the souls out of one another; and in place of sixty brisk useful craftsmen, the world has sixty dead carcasses, which it must bury, and anew shed tears for. Had these men any quarrel? Busy as the Devil is, not the smallest! They lived far enough apart; were the entirest strangers; nay, in so wide a Universe, there was even unconsciously, by Commerce, some mutual helpfulness between them. How then? Simpleton! their Governors had fallen-out; and, instead of shooting one another, had the cunning to make these poor blockheads shoot.—Alas, so is it in Deutschland, and hitherto in all other lands; still as of old, 'what devilry soever Kings do, the Greeks must pay the piper!'—In that fiction of the English Smollett, it is true, the final Cessation of War is perhaps prophetically shadowed forth; where the two Natural

Enemies, in person, take each a Tobacco-pipe, filled
with Brimstone; light the same, and smoke in one
another's faces till the weaker gives in: but from
such predicted Peace-Era, what blood-filled trenches,
and contentious centuries, may still divide us!' "

The chapter called "The Everlasting Yea" (Book
2, Chapter 9) is, as we have already seen in the
quotation from Carlyle's *Reminiscences,* a transcript
of his own experience in the summer of 1825.

The Everlasting Yea

" 'Beautiful it was to sit there, as in my skyey
Tent, musing and meditating; on the high table-land,
in front of the Mountains; over me, as roof, the
azure Dome, and around me, for walls, four azure-
flowing curtains,—namely, of the Four azure Winds,
on whose bottom-fringes also I have seen gilding.
And then to fancy the fair Castles, that stood sheltered in these Mountain hollows; with their green
flower-lawns, and white dames and damosels, lovely
enough: or better still, the straw-roofed Cottages,
wherein stood many a Mother baking bread, with
her children round her:—all hidden and protect-
ingly folded up in the valley-folds; yet there and

alive, as sure as if I beheld them. Or to see, as well
as fancy, the nine Towns and Villages, that lay
round my mountain-seat, which, in still weather,
were wont to speak to me (by their steeple-bells)
with metal tongue; and, in almost all weather, pro-
claimed their vitality by repeated Smoke-clouds;
whereon, as on a culinary horologue, I might read
the hour of the day. For it was the smoke of cook-
ery, as kind housewives at morning, mid-day, even-
tide, were boiling their husbands' kettles; and ever
a blue pillar rose up into the air, successively or
simultaneously, from each of the nine, saying, as
plainly as smoke could say: Such and such a meal
is getting ready here. Not uninteresting! For you
have the whole Borough, with all its love-makings
and scandal-mongeries, contentions and content-
ments, as in miniature, and could cover it all with
your hat.—If, in my wide Wayfarings, I had
learned to look into the business of the World in
its details, here perhaps was the place for combining
it into general propositions, and deducing inferences
therefrom.

" 'Often also I could see the black Tempest
marching in anger through the distance: round some
Schreckhorn, as yet grim-blue, would the eddying

vapour gather, and there tumultuously eddy, and flow down like a mad witch's hair; till, after a space, it vanished, and, in the clear sunbeam, your Schreckhorn stood smiling grim-white, for the vapour had held snow. How thou fermentest and elaboratest in thy great fermenting-vat and laboratory of an Atmosphere, of a World, O Nature!—Or what is Nature? Ha! why do I not name thee GOD? Art thou not the 'Living Garment of God'? O Heavens, is it, in very deed, HE, then, that ever speaks through thee; that lives and loves in thee, that lives and loves in me?

" 'Fore-shadows, call them rather fore-splendours, of that Truth, and Beginning of Truths, fell mysteriously over my soul. Sweeter than Dayspring to the Shipwrecked in Nova Zembla; ah, like the mother's voice to her little child that strays bewildered, weeping, in unknown tumults; like soft streamings of celestial music to my too-exasperated heart, came that Evangel. The Universe is not dead and demoniacal, a charnel-house with spectres; but godlike, and my Father's!

" 'With other eyes, too, could I now look upon my fellow man: with an infinite Love, an infinite Pity. Poor, wandering, wayward man! Art thou not tried,

and beaten with stripes, even as I am? Ever,
whether thou bear the royal mantle or the beggar's
gabardine, art thou not so weary, so heavy-laden;
and thy Bed of Rest is but a Grave. O my Brother,
my Brother, why can not I shelter thee in my bosom,
and wipe away all tears from thy eyes!—Truly, the
din of many-voiced Life, which, in this solitude,
with the mind's organ, I could hear, was no longer
a maddening discord, but a melting one; like inarticulate cries, and sobbings of a dumb creature,
which in the ear of Heaven are prayers. The poor
Earth, with her poor joys, was now my needy
Mother, not my cruel Stepdame; Man, with his so
mad Wants and so mean Endeavours, had become
the dearer to me; and even for his sufferings and
his sins, I now first named him Brother. Thus was
I standing in the porch of that *"Sanctuary of Sorrow;"* by strange, steep ways, had I too been guided
thither; and ere long its sacred gates would open,
and the *"Divine Depth of Sorrow"* lie disclosed to
me.'

"The Professor says, he here first got eye on the
Knot that had been strangling him, and straightway
could unfasten it, and was free. 'A vain intermina-
ble controversy,' writes he, 'touching what is at

present called Origin of Evil, or some such thing,
arises in every soul, since the beginning of the
world; and in every soul, that would pass from idle
Suffering into actual Endeavouring, must first be
put an end to. The most, in our time, have to go
content with a simple, incomplete enough Suppres-
sion of this controversy; to a few, some Solution
of it is indispensable. In every new era, too, such
Solution comes-out in different terms; and ever the
Solution of the last era has become obsolete, and is
found unserviceable. For it is man's nature to
change his Dialect from century to century; he can
not help it though he would. The authentic *Church-
Catechism* of our present century has not yet fallen
into my hands: meanwhile, for my own private be-
hoof, I attempt to elucidate the matter so. Man's
Unhappiness, as I construe, comes of his Greatness;
it is because there is an Infinite in him, which with
all his cunning he can not quite bury under the
Finite. Will the whole Finance Ministers and Up-
holsterers and Confectioners of modern Europe undertake, in joint-stock company, to make one Shoeblack HAPPY? They can not accomplish it, above
an hour or two: for the Shoeblack also has a Soul
quite other than his Stomach; and would require, if

you consider it, for his permanent satisfaction and saturation, simply this allotment, no more, and no less: *God's infinite Universe altogether to himself,* therein to enjoy infinitely, and fill every wish as fast as it rose. Oceans of Hochheimer, a Throat like that of Ophiuchus: speak not of them; to the infinite Shoeblack they are as nothing. No sooner is your ocean filled, than he grumbles that it might have been of better vintage. Try him with half of a Universe, of an Omnipotence, he sets to quarrelling with the proprietor of the other half, and declares himself the most maltreated of men.—Always there is a black spot in our sunshine: it is even, as I said, the *Shadow of Ourselves.*

" 'But the whim we have of Happiness is somewhat thus. By certain valuations, and averages, of our own striking, we come upon some sort of average terrestrial lot; this we fancy belongs to us by nature, and of indefeasible right. It is simple payment of our wages, of our deserts; requires neither thanks nor complaint; only such *overplus* as there may be do we account Happiness; any *deficit* again is Misery. Now consider that we have the valuation of our own deserts ourselves, and what a fund of Self-conceit there is in each of us,—do you wonder that the balance should so often dip the wrong way, and many a Blockhead cry: See there, what a payment; was ever worthy gentleman so used!—I tell thee, Blockhead, it all comes of thy Vanity; of what thou *fanciest* those same deserts of thine to be. Fancy that thou deservest to be hanged (as is most likely), thou wilt feel it happiness to be only shot: fancy that thou deservest to be hanged in a hair-halter, it will be a luxury to die in hemp.

" 'So true it is, what I then said, that *the Fraction of Life can be increased in value not so much by increasing your Numerator as by lessening your Denominator*. Nay, unless my Algebra deceive me, *Unity* itself divided by *Zero* will give *Infinity*. Make thy claim of wages a zero, then; thou hast the world under thy feet. Well did the Wisest of our time write: 'It is only with Renunciation (*Entsagen*) that Life, properly speaking, can be said to begin.'

" 'I asked myself: What is this that, ever since earliest years, thou hast been fretting and fuming, and lamenting and self-tormenting, on account of? Say it in a word: is it not because thou art not HAPPY? Because the THOU (sweet gentleman) is not sufficiently honoured, nourished, soft-bedded, and lovingly cared for? Foolish soul! What act of

Legislature was there that *thou* shouldst be Happy?
A little while ago thou hadst no right to *be* at all.
What if thou wert born and predestined not to be
Happy, but to be Unhappy! Art thou nothing other
than a Vulture, then, that fliest through the Uni-
verse seeking after somewhat to *eat;* and shrieking
dolefully because carrion enough is not given thee?
Close thy *Byron;* open thy *Goethe.'*

" '*Es leuchtet mir ein,* I see a glimpse of it!' cries
he elsewhere: 'there is in man a HIGHER than Love
of Happiness: he can do without Happiness, and instead thereof find Blessedness! Was it not to
preach-forth this same HIGHER that sages and martyrs, the Poet and the Priest, in all times, have
spoken and suffered; bearing testimony, through
life and through death, of the Godlike that is in
Man, and how in the Godlike only has he Strength
and Freedom? Which God-inspired Doctrine art
thou also honoured to be taught; O Heavens! and
broken with manifold merciful Afflictions, even till
thou become contrite, and learn it! O, thank thy
Destiny for these; thankfully bear what yet remain:
thou hadst need of them; the Self in thee needed to
be annihilated. By benignant fever-paroxysms is
Life rooting out the deep-seated chronic Disease,

and triumphs over Death. On the roaring billows of Time, thou art not engulfed, but borne aloft into the azure of Eternity. Love not Pleasure; love God. This is the EVERLASTING YEA, wherein all contradiction is solved: wherein whoso walks and works, it is well with him.' "

Finally, from the chapter entitled "Natural Supernaturalism" (Book 3, Chapter 9) let us choose the magnificent prose-poem which embodies the central metaphor of *Sartor Resartus*.

The Illusions of Space and Time

" 'But the deepest of all illusory Appearances, for hiding Wonder, as for many other ends, are your two grand fundamental world-enveloping Appearances, SPACE and TIME. These, as spun and woven for us from before Birth itself, to clothe our celestial ME for dwelling here, and yet blind to it,— lie all-embracing, as the universal canvas, or warp and woof, whereby all minor Illusions, in this Phantasm Existence, weave and paint themselves. In vain, while here on Earth, shall you endeavour to strip them off; you can, at best, but rend them asunder for moments, and look through.

" 'Fortunatus had a wishing Hat, which when he put on, and wished himself Anywhere, behold he was There. By this means had Fortunatus triumphed over Space, he had annihilated Space; for him there was no Where, but all was Here. Were a Hatter to establish himself, in the Wahngasse of Weissnichtwo, and make felts of this sort for all mankind, what a world we should have of it! Still stranger, on the opposite side of the street, another Hatter establish himself; and, as his fellow-craftsman made Space-annihilating Hats, make Time-annihilating! Of both would I purchase, were it with my last groschen; but chiefly of this latter. To clap-on your felt, and, simply by wishing that you were Any*where,* straightway to be *There!* Next to clap-on your other felt, and simply by wishing that you were Any*when,* and straightway to be *Then!* This were indeed the grander: shooting at will from the Fire-Creation of the World to its Fire-Consummation; here historically present in the First Century, conversing face to face with Paul and Seneca; there prophetically in the Thirty-first, conversing also face to face with other Pauls and Senecas, who as yet stand hidden in the depth of that late Time!

" 'Or thinkest thou, it were impossible, unimag-

inable? Is the Past annihilated, then, or only past;
is the Future non-extant or only future? Those
mystic faculties of thine, Memory and Hope, already
answer: already through those mystic avenues, thou
the Earth-blinded summonest both Past and Future,
and communest with them, though as yet darkly,
and with mute beckonings. The curtains of Yesterday drop down, the curtains of Tomorrow roll up;
but Yesterday and Tomorrow both *are*. Pierce
through the Time-Element, glance into the Eternal.
Believe what thou findest written in the sanctuaries
of Man's Soul, even as all Thinkers, in all ages,
have devoutly read it there: that Time and Space
are not God, but creations of God; that with God
as it is a universal HERE, so it is an everlasting NOW.

" 'And seest thou therein any glimpse of IMMOR-
TALITY?—O Heaven! Is the white Tomb of our
Loved One, who died from our arms, and had to be
left behind us there, which rises in the distance, like
a pale, mournfully receding Milestone, to tell how
many toilsome uncheered miles we have journeyed
on alone,—but a pale spectral Illusion! Is the lost
Friend still mysteriously Here, even as we are Here
mysteriously, with God!—Know of a truth that only
the Time-shadows have perished, or are perishable;

that the real Being of whatever was, and whatever
is, and whatever will be, *is* even now and forever.
This, should it unhappily seem new, thou mayst pon-
der at thy leisure; for the next twenty years, or the
next twenty centuries: believe it thou must; understand it thou canst not.

"'That the Thought-forms, Space and Time,
wherein, once for all, we are sent into this Earth to
live, should condition and determine our whole Practical reasonings, conceptions, and imagings or imag-
inings—seems altogether fit, just, and unavoidable.
But that they should, furthermore, usurp such sway
over pure spiritual Meditation, and blind us to the
wonder everywhere lying close on us, seems nowise
so. Admit Space and Time to their due rank as
Forms of Thought; nay, even, if thou wilt, to their
quite undue rank of Realities: and consider, then,
with thyself how their thin disguises hide from us
the brightest God-effulgences! Thus, were it not
miraculous, could I stretch forth my hand, and
clutch the Sun? Yet thou seest me daily stretch
forth my hand and therewith clutch many a thing,
and swing it hither and thither. Art thou a grown
baby, then, to fancy that the Miracle lies in miles of
distance, or in pounds avoirdupois of weight; and

not to see that the true inexplicable God-revealing
Miracle lies in this, that I can stretch forth my hand
at all; that I have free Force to clutch aught therewith? Innumerable other of this sort are the decep-
tions, and wonder-hiding stupefactions, which Space
practises on us.

" 'Still worse is it with regard to Time. Your
grand anti-magician, and universal wonder-hider, is
this same lying Time. Had we but the Time-annihilating Hat, to put on for once only, we should see
ourselves in a World of Miracles, wherein all fabled
or authentic Thaumaturgy, and feats of Magic,
were outdone. But unhappily we have not such a
Hat; and man, poor fool that he is, can seldom and
scantily help himself without one.

" 'Were it not wonderful, for instance, had Orpheus, or Amphion, built the walls of Thebes by
the mere sound of his Lyre? Yet tell me, Who built
these walls of Weissnichtwo; summoning out all the
sandstone rocks, to dance along from the *Steinbruch*
(now a huge Troglodyte Chasm, with frightful
green-mantled pools); and shape themselves into
Doric and Ionic pillars, squared ashlar houses, and
noble streets? Was it not the still higher Orpheus,
or Orpheuses, who, in past centuries, by the divine

Music of Wisdom, succeeded in civilising man? Our
highest Orpheus walked in Judea, eighteen hundred
years ago: his sphere-melody, flowing in wild native
tones, took captive the ravished souls of men; and
being of a truth sphere-melody, still flows and
sounds, though now with thousandfold accompani-
ments, and rich symphonies, through all our hearts;
and modulates, and divinely leads them. Is that a
wonder, which happens in two hours; and does it
cease to be wonderful if happening in two million?
Not only was Thebes built by the music of an Orpheus; but without the music of some inspired Orpheus was no city ever built, no work that man
glories in ever done.

" 'Sweep away the Illusion of Time; glance, if
thou have eyes, from the near moving-cause to its
far-distant Mover: The stroke that came transmit-
ted through a whole galaxy of elastic balls, was it
less a stroke than if the last ball only had been
struck, and sent flying? O, could I (with the Time-
annihilating Hat) transport thee direct from the
Beginnings to the Endings, how were thy eyesight
unsealed, and thy heart set flaming in the Light-sea
of celestial wonder! Then sawest thou that this
fair Universe, were it in the meanest province

thereof, is in very deed the star-domed City of God;
that through every star, through every grass-blade,
and most through every Living Soul, the glory of a
present God still beams. But Nature, which is the
Time-vesture of God, and reveals Him to the wise,
hides Him from the foolish.

" 'Again, could anything be more miraculous than
an actual authentic Ghost? The English Johnson
longed, all his life, to see one; but could not, though
he went to Cock Lane, and thence to the church-
vaults, and tapped on coffins. Foolish Doctor! Did
he never, with the mind's eye as well as with the
body's, look round him into that full tide of human
Life he so loved; did he never so much as look into
Himself? The good Doctor was a Ghost, as actual
and authentic as heart could wish; well-nigh a million of Ghosts were travelling the streets by his side.
Once more I say, sweep away the illusion of Time;
compress the threescore years into three minutes:
what else was he, what else are we? Are we not
Spirits, that are shaped into a body, into an Appearance; and that fade away again into air and Invisi-
bility? This is no metaphor, it is a simple, scientific
fact: we start out of Nothingness, take figure, and
are Apparitions; round us, as round the veriest

spectre, is Eternity; and to Eternity minutes are as years and æons. Come there not tones of Love and Faith, as from celestial harp-strings, like the Song of beatified Souls? And again, do not we squeak and gibber (in our discordant, screech-owlish debatings and recriminatings); and glide bodeful and feeble, and fearful; or uproar (*poltern*), and revel in our mad Dance of the Dead,—till the scent of the morning-air summons us to our still Home; and dreamy Night becomes awake and Day? Where now is Alexander of Macedon: does the steel Host, that yelled in fierce battle-shouts at Issus and Arbela, remain behind him; or have they all vanished utterly, even as perturbed Goblins must? Napoleon too, and his Moscow Retreats and Austerlitz Campaigns! Was it all other than the veriest Spectre-hunt; which has now, with its howling tumult that made night hideous, flitted away?—Ghosts! There are nigh a thousand-million walking the Earth openly at noontide; some half-hundred have vanished from it, some half-hundred have arisen in it, ere thy watch ticks once.

" 'O Heaven, it is mysterious, it is awful to consider that we not only carry each a future Ghost within him; but are, in very deed, Ghosts! These

Limbs, whence had we them; this stormy Force;
this life-blood with its burning Passion? They are
dust and shadow; a Shadow-system gathered round
our ME; wherein through some moments or years,
the Divine Essence is to be revealed in the Flesh.
That warrior on his strong war-horse, fire flashes
through his eyes; force dwells in his arm and heart;
but warrior and war-horse are a vision; a revealed
Force, nothing more. Stately they tread the Earth,
as if it were a firm substance: fool! the Earth is
but a film; it cracks in twain, and warrior and war-
horse sink beyond plummet's sounding. Plummet's?
Fantasy herself will not follow them. A little while
ago they were not; a little while, and they are not,
their very ashes are not.

" 'So it has been from the beginning, so it will be
to the end. Generation after generation takes to
itself the Form of a Body; and forth-issuing from
Cimmerian Night, on Heaven's mission APPEARS.
What Force and Fire is in each he expends: one
grinding in the mill of Industry; one hunter-like
climbing the giddy Alpine heights of Science; one
madly dashed in pieces on the rocks of Strife, in
war with his fellow:—and then the Heaven-sent is
recalled; his earthly Vesture falls away, and soon

even to Sense becomes a vanished Shadow. Thus,
like some wild-flaming, wild-thundering train of
Heaven's Artillery, does this mysterious MANKIND
thunder and flame, in long-drawn, quick-succeeding
grandeur, through the unknown Deep. Thus, like
a God-created, fire-breathing Spirit-host, we
emerge from the Inane; haste stormfully across the
astonished Earth; then plunge again into the Inane.
Earth's mountains are levelled, and her seas filled
up, in our passage: can the Earth, which is but
dead and a vision, resist Spirits which have reality
and are alive? On the hardest adamant some footprint of us is stamped-in; the last Rear of the host
will read traces of the earliest Van. But whence?—
O Heaven, whither? Sense knows not; Faith knows
not; only that it is through Mystery to Mystery,
from God and to God.

> " ' "We *are such stuff*
> As Dreams are made on, and our little Life
> Is rounded with a sleep!" ' "

CHAPTER XI

THE FRENCH REVOLUTION

WE HAVE already touched upon Carlyle's artistic aim in writing his *French Revolution,* and have examined briefly his manner of composition. Before presenting some typical passages, let us review, in Garnett's words, the method followed in this most individual of all historical writings.

"To give Carlyle's method the briefest possible definition, were perhaps to say that he strove to write history in the study as he would have reported it in the street. He relied upon personal memoirs, to a degree unusual even in a historian of France. While other historians had sought to blend these details into a smooth equable narrative, as rags are fashioned into a sheet of paper, Carlyle took the rags themselves and hung them forth gay or grimy or blood-stained, dancing in air or trailing in mud. Other historians gave the Revolution at second-hand, but he at first-hand. That peculiar feeling of reality, as if one's own blood bounded with the emotion of the event, which others have successfully called up in detached scenes, as Schiller in his description of the battle of Lutzen, Carlyle excited throughout a long history. The secret was his power of such thorough identification with the feelings of the actors in the occurrences that the reader felt a witness, and the witness seemed well-nigh an actor in the impassioned drama.

"This power was not peculiar to Carlyle, it belongs more or less to all poets and novelists who excel in the delineation of action. He had, however, a great advantage over most poets and novelists in his intense penetration with his subject. He wrote less as an artist than as a prophet. He believed that the French Revolution was the living manifestation of the truths he held most dear. The sublimity of fact, the impotence of phrase, the folly of formula, the loathsomeness of rotten institutions, the reeling frenzy of the unguided multitude, the saving virtue of efficiency, that salt of scoundrelism; these things he saw written throughout the whole eventful history. He need not, as in *Sartor,* spin his argument from his own brain, the facts would preach

eloquently enough.   He was fortunate moreover in
a subject which exactly fitted his style.   Vividness
is always a precious quality, yet some incongruity
must have been felt if the tale of ancient Greece or
modern Italy had been told in the language of *The
French Revolution*.   Nor could such a style have
been proper or even practicable where the element of first-hand testimony was less prepondera-
ting.   But the French Revolution was volcanic
enough to justify Carlylese vehemence of treatment;
and its archives, whether extant in contemporary
pamphlets or in memoirs, were the work of those
who spoke of what they knew and testified of what
they had seen."

Carlyle's ethical purpose, in this book, is as indubitable as his technical performance.   It has been
expounded by Froude in one of his finest chapters
(*Carlyle's Life in London,* I. 4) from which we
may borrow a few sentences:

". . . Struggling thus in pain and sorrow, he
desired to tell the modern world that, destitute as it
and its affairs appeared to be of Divine guidance,
God or justice was still in the middle of it, sternly
inexorable as ever; that modern nations were as entirely governed by God's law as the Israelites had

been in Palestine—laws self-acting and inflicting their own penalties, if man neglected or defied them. And these laws were substantially the same as those on the Tables delivered in thunder on Mount Sinai. You shall reverence your Almighty Maker. You shall speak the truth. You shall do justice to your fellow-man. If you set truth aside for conventional and convenient lies; if you prefer your own pleasure, your own will, your own ambition, to purity and manliness and justice, and submission to your Maker's commands, then are whirlwinds still provided in the constitution of things which will blow you to atoms. Philistines, Assyrians, Babylonians, were the whips which were provided for the Israelites. Germans and Huns swept away the Roman sensualists. Modern society, though out of fear of barbarian conquerors, breeds in its own heart the instruments of its punishment. The hungry and injured millions will rise up and bring to justice their guilty rulers, themselves little better than those whom they throw down, themselves powerless to rebuild out of the ruins any abiding city; but powerful to destroy, powerful to dash in pieces the corrupt institutions which have been the shelter and the instrument of oppression.

"And Carlyle *believed* this—believed it singly and simply as Isaiah believed it, not as a mode of speech to be used in pulpits by eloquent preachers, but as actual literal fact, as a real account of the true living relations between man and Maker. The established forms, creeds, liturgies, articles of faith, were but as the shell round the kernel. The shell in these days of ours had rotted away, and men supposed that, because the shell was gone, the entire conception had been but a dream. It was no dream. The kernel could not rot. It was the vital force by which human existence in this planet was controlled, and would be controlled to the end."

To these comments upon the artistic and moral intention of *The French Revolution* little needs to be added, except a single caution to the reader. He ought, in order to enjoy the book to the full, to know the main facts of the Revolution in advance. Carlyle's method requires that the reader shall meet the author half-way,—and often more than half-way. Carlyle takes for granted that we are already acquainted with the chief events under consideration. He also presupposes that we possess a certain degree of imaginative power, and that we are willing to read dynamically and not passively. Unless we are able and willing to conform to such conditions, it is useless to approach this masterpiece.

Perhaps its distinctive qualities are to be most clearly grasped in the description of a few events and in the characterization of certain persons.

Death of Louis XV

"Frightful to all men is Death; from of old named King of Terrors. Our little compact home of an Existence, where we dwelt complaining, yet as in a home, is passing, in dark agonies, into an Unknown of Separation, Foreignness, unconditioned Possibility. The Heathen Emperor asks of his soul: Into what places art thou now departing? The Catholic King must answer: To the Judgment-bar of the Most High God! Yes, it is a summing up of Life; a final settling, and giving-in the 'account of the deeds done in the body:' they are done now; and lie there unalterable, and do bear their fruits, long as Eternity shall last.

"Louis XV had always the kingliest abhorrence of Death. Unlike that praying Duke of Orleans, *Egalite's* grandfather,—for indeed several of them had a touch of madness,—who honestly believed that there was no Death! He, if the Court News-

men can be believed, started up once on a time,
glowing with sulphurous contempt and indignation
on his poor Secretary, who had stumbled on the
words, *feu roi d'Espagne* (the late King of Spain) :
'*Feu roi, Monsieur?*'—'Monseigneur,' hastily answered the trembling but adroit man of business,
'*c'est une titre qu'ils prennent* ('tis a title they
take).' Louis, we say, was not so happy; but he did
what he could. He would not suffer Death to be
spoken of; avoided the sight of churchyards, fu-
nereal monuments, and whatsoever could bring it
to mind. It is the resource of the Ostrich; who,
hard hunted, sticks his foolish head in the ground,
and would fain forget that his foolish unseeing
body is not unseen too. Or sometimes, with a spas-
modic antagonism, significant of the same thing, and
of more, he *would* go; or stopping his court car-
riages, would send into churchyards, and ask 'how
many new graves there were to-day,' though it gave
his poor Pompadour the disagreeablest qualms. We
can figure the thought of Louis that day, when, all
royally caparisoned for hunting, he met, at some
sudden turning in the Wood of Senart, a ragged
Peasant with a coffin: 'For whom?'—It was for a
poor brother slave, whom Majesty had sometimes

noticed slaving in those quarters: 'What did he die
of?'—'Of hunger:'—the King gave his steed the
spur.

"But figure his thought, when Death is now
clutching at his own heart-strings; unlooked for,
inexorable! Yes, poor Louis, Death has found thee.
No palace walls or life-guards, gorgeous tapestries
or gilt buckram of stiffest ceremonial could keep
him out; but he is here, here at thy very life-breath,
and will extinguish it. Thou, whose whole existence
hitherto was a chimera and scenic show, at length
becomest a reality: sumptuous Versailles bursts
asunder, like a dream, into void Immensity; Time
is done, and all the scaffolding of Time falls wrecked
with hideous clangour round thy soul: the pale King-
doms yawn open; there must thou enter, naked, all
unking'd, and await what is appointed thee! Unhappy man, there as thou turnest, in dull agony, on
thy bed of weariness, what a thought is thine! Pur-
gatory and Hell-fire, now all too possible, in the
prospect: in the retrospect—alas, what thing didst
thou do that were not better undone; what mortal
didst thou generously help; what sorrow hadst thou
mercy on? Do the 'five hundred thousand' ghosts,
who sank shamefully on so many battle-fields from

Rossbach to Quebec, that thy Harlot might take re-
venge for an epigram,—crowd round thee in this
hour? Thy foul Harem; the curses of mothers,
the tears and infamy of daughters? Miserable man!
thou 'hast done evil as thou couldst :' thy whole existence seems one hideous abortion and mistake of
Nature; the use and meaning of thee not yet known.
Wert thou a fabulous Griffin, *devouring* the works
of men; daily dragging virgins to thy cave;—clad
also in scales that no spear would pierce : no spear
but Death's? A Griffin not fabulous but real!
Frightful, O Louis, seem these moments for thee.—
We will pry no further into the horrors of a sin-
ner's deathbed."

Fall of the Bastille

"To describe the Scige of the Bastille (thought to
be one of the most important in History) perhaps
transcends the talent of mortals. Could one but,
after infinite reading, get to understand so much as
the plan of the building! But there is open Esplanade, at the end of the Rue Saint-Antoine;
there are such Forecourts, *Cour Avancé, Cour de
l'Orme,* arched Gateway (where Louis Tournay
now fights); then new drawbridges, dormant-

bridges, rampart-bastions, and the grim Eight
Towers: a labyrinthic Mass, high-frowning there,
of all ages from twenty years to four hundred and
twenty;—beleaguered, in this its last hour, as we
said, by mere Chaos come again! Ordnance of all
calibres; throats of all capacities; men of all plans,
every man his own engineer: seldom since the war
of Pygmies and Cranes was there seen so anom-
alous a thing. Half-pay Elie is home for a suit
of regimentals; no one would heed him in coloured
clothes: half-pay Hulin is haranguing Gardes Françaises in the Place de Grève. Frantic Patriots pick
up the grapeshots; bear them, still hot (or seem-
ingly so), to the Hôtel-de-Ville:—Paris, you perceive, is to be burnt! Flesselles is 'pale to the very
lips,' for the roar of the multitude grows deep.
Paris wholly has got to the acme of its frenzy;
whirled, all ways, by panic madness. At every street
barricade, there whirls simmering a minor whirl-
pool,—strengthening the barricade, since God knows
what is coming; and all minor whirlpools play dis-
tractedly into that grand Fire-Mahlstrom which is
lashing round the Bastille.

"And so it lashes and it roars. Cholat the wine-
merchant has become an impromptu cannoneer. See

Georget, of the Marine Service, fresh from Brest, ply the King of Siam's cannon. Singular (if we were not used to the like) : Georget lay, last night, taking his ease at his inn; the King of Siam's cannon also lay, knowing nothing of *him,* for a hundred years. Yet now at the right instant, they have got together, and discourse eloquent music. For, hearing what was toward, Georget sprang from the Brest Diligence, and ran. Gardes Françaises also will be here, with real artillery: were not the walls so thick!—Upwards from the Esplanade, horizontally from all neighbouring roofs and windows, flashes one irregular deluge of musketry, without effect. The Invalides lie flat, firing comparatively at their ease from behind stone; hardly through portholes, show the tip of a nose. We fall, shot; and make no impression!

"Let conflagrations rage; of whatsoever is combustible! Guard-rooms are burnt, Invalides messrooms. A distracted 'Peruke-maker with two fiery torches' is for burning 'the saltpetres of the Arsenal;'—had not a woman run screaming; had not a Patriot, with some tincture of Natural Philosophy, instantly struck the wind out of him (butt of musket on pit of stomach)', overturned barrels, and stayed the devouring element. A young beautiful lady, seized escaping in these Outer Courts, and thought falsely to be De Launay's daughter, shall be burnt in De Launay's sight; she lies swooned on a paillasse: but again a Patriot, it is brave Aubin Bonnemère the old soldier, dashes in, and rescues her. Straw is burnt; three cartloads of it, hauled thither, go up in white smoke: almost to the choking of Patriotism itself; so that Elie had, with singed brows, to drag back one cart; and Réole, the 'gigantic haberdasher' another. Smoke as of Tophet; confusion as of Babel; noise as of the Crack of Doom!

"Blood flows; the aliment of new madness. The wounded are carried into houses of the Rue Cerisaie; the dying leave their last mandate not to yield till the accursed Stronghold fall. And yet, alas, how fall? The walls are so thick! Deputations, three in number, arrive from the Hôtel-de-Ville; Abbé Fauchet (who was of one) can say, with what almost superhuman courage of benevolence. These wave their Town-flag in the arched Gateway; and stand, rolling their drum; but to no purpose. In such Crack of Doom, De Launay can not hear them, dare not believe them: they return, with justified rage, the whew of lead still singing in their ears. What to do? The Firemen are here, squirting with their fire-pumps on the Invalides cannon, to wet the touchholes; they unfortunately can not squirt so high; but produce only clouds of spray. Individuals of classical knowledge propose *catapults*. Santerre, the sonorous Brewer of the Suburb Saint-Antoine, advises rather that the place be fired, by a 'mixture of phosphorous and oil-of-turpentine spouted up through forcing pumps:' O Spinola-Santerre, hast thou the mixture *ready?* Every man his own engineer! And still the fire-deluge abates not: even women are firing, and Turks; at least one woman (with her sweetheart) and one Turk. Gardes Françaises have come: real cannon, real cannoneers. Usher Maillard is busy; half-pay Elie, half-pay Hulin rage in the midst of thousands.

"How the great Bastille Clock ticks (inaudible) in its Inner Court there, at its ease, hour after hour; as if nothing special, for it or the world, were passing! It tolled One when the firing began; and is now pointing towards Five, and still the firing slakes not.—Far down, in their vaults, the seven Prisoners hear muffled din as of earthquakes; their Turnkeys answer vaguely.

"Wo to thee, De Launay, with thy poor hundred Invalides! Broglie is distant, and his ears heavy: Besenval hears, but can send no help. One poor troop of Hussars has crept, reconnoitering, cautiously along the Quais, as far as the Pont Neuf. 'We are come to join you,' said the Captain; for the crowd seems shoreless. A large-headed dwarfish individual, of smoke-bleared aspect, shambles forward, opening his blue lips, for there is sense in him; and croaks: 'Alight then, and give up your arms!' The Hussar-Captain is too happy to be escorted to the Barriers, and dismissed on parole. Who the squat individual was? Men answer, It is M. Marat, author of the excellent pacific *Avis au Peuple!* Great truly, O thou remarkable Dog-leech, is this thy day of emergence and new-birth; and yet this same day come four years——!—But let the curtains of the Future hang.

"What shall De Launay do? One thing only De Launay could have done: what he said he would do. Fancy him sitting, from the first with lighted taper, within arm's length of the Powder-Magazine; motionless, like old Roman Senator, or Bronze Lamp-holder; coldly apprising Thuriot, and all men, by a slight motion of his eye, what his resolution was:

—Harmless he sat there, while unharmed; but the King's Fortress, meanwhile, could, might, would, or should, in nowise be surrendered, save to the King's Messenger: one old man's life is worthless, so it be lost with honour; but think, ye brawling *canaille,* how it will be when a whole Bastille springs skyward!—In such statuesque, taper-holding attitude, one fancies De Launay might have left Thuriot, the red Clerks of the Basoche, Curé of Saint-Stephen and all the tag-rag-and-bobtail of the world, to work their will.

"And yet, withal, he could not do it. Hast thou considered how each man's heart is so tremulously responsive to the hearts of all men; hast thou noted how omnipotent is the very sound of many men? How their shriek of indignation palsies the strong soul; their howl of contumely withers with unfelt pangs? The Ritter Gluck confessed that the ground-tone of the noblest passage, in one of his noblest Operas, was the voice of the Populace he had heard at Vienna, crying to their Kaiser: Bread! Bread! Great is the combined voice of men; the utterance of their *instincts* which are truer than their *thoughts:* it is the greatest a man encounters, among the sounds and shadows which make up this World of

Time.   He who can resist that, has his footing
somewhere *beyond* Time.   De Launay could not do
it.   Distracted, he hovers between two; hopes in
the middle of despair; surrenders not his Fortress;
declares that he will blow it up, seizes torches to
blow it up, and does not blow it.   Unhappy old De
Launay, it is the death-agony of thy Bastille and
thee!   Jail, Jailoring and Jailor, all three, such as
they may have been, must finish.

"For four hours now has the World-Bedlam
roared: call it the World-Chimæra, blowing fire!
The poor Invalides have sunk their battlements, or
rise only with reversed muskets: they have made a
white flag of napkins; go beating the *chamade,* or
seeming to beat, for one can hear nothing.   The
very Swiss at the Portcullis look weary of firing;
disheartened in the fire-deluge: a porthole at the
drawbridge is opened, as by one that would speak.
See Huissier Maillard, the shifty man!   On his
plank, swinging over the abyss of that stone Ditch;
plank resting on a parapet, balanced by weight of
Patriots,—he hovers perilous: such a Dove towards such an Ark!   Deftly, thou shifty Usher: one
man already fell; and lies smashed, far down there,
against the masonry; Usher Maillard falls not:

deftly, unerring he walks, with outspread palm. The
Swiss holds a paper through his porthole; the shifty
Usher snatches it, and returns. Terms of surrender:
Pardon, immunity to all! Are they accepted?—'*Foi
d'officier,* On the word of an officer,' answers half-
pay Hulin,—or half-pay Elie, for men do not agree
on it, 'they are!' Sinks the drawbridge,—Usher
Maillard bolting it when down; rushes-in the living
deluge: the Bastille is fallen! *Victoire! La Bastille
est prise!*

Execution of Louis XVI

"To this conclusion, then, hast thou come, O hapless Louis! The Son of Sixty Kings is to die on
the Scaffold by form of Law. Under Sixty Kings
this same form of Law, form of Society, has been
fashioning itself together, these thousand years;
and has become, one way and other, a most strange
Machine. Surely, if needful, it is also frightful, this
Machine; dead, blind; not what it should be; which,
with swift stroke, or by cold slow torture, has wasted
the lives and souls of innumerable men. And behold now a King himself, or say rather Knighthood
in his person, is to expire here in cruel tortures;—
like a Phalaris shut in the belly of his own red-

heated Brazen Bull! It is ever so; and thou shouldst
know it, O haughty tyrannous man: injustice breeds
injustice; curses and falsehoods do verily return 'always *home,'* wide as they may wander.   Innocent
Louis bears the sins of many generations: he too
experiences that man's tribunal is not in this Earth;
that if he had no Higher one, it were not well with
him.

"A King dying by such violence appeals impres-
sively to the imagination; as the like must do, and
ought to do.   And yet at bottom it is not the King
dying, but the man! Kingship is a coat: the grand
loss is of the skin.   The man from whom you take
his Life, to him can the whole combined world do
more?   Lally went on his hurdle; his mouth filled
with a gag.   Miserablest mortals, doomed for pick-
ing pockets, have a whole five-act Tragedy in them,
in that dumb pain, as they go to the gallows, unre-
garded; they consume the cup of trembling down to
the lees.   For Kings and for Beggars, for the justly
doomed and the unjustly, it is a hard thing to die.
Pity them all: thy utmost pity, with all aids and ap-
pliances and throne-and-scaffold contrasts, how far
short is it of the thing pitied!

"A Confessor has come; Abbé Edgeworth, of

Irish extraction, whom the King knew by good report, has come promptly on this solemn mission. Leave the Earth alone, then, thou hapless King; it with its malice will go its way, thou also canst go thine. A hard scene yet remains: the parting with our loved ones. Kind hearts, environed in the same grim peril with us; to be left *here*! Let the Reader look with the eyes of Valet Cléry, through these glass-doors, where also the Municipality watches; and see the cruellest of scenes:

" 'At half-past eight, the door of the ante-room opened: the Queen appeared first, leading her Son by the hand; then Madame Royale and Madame Elizabeth: they all flung themselves into the arms of the King. Silence reigned for some minutes: interrupted only by sobs. The Queen made a movement to lead his Majesty towards the inner room, where M. Edgeworth was waiting unknown to them: 'No,' said the King, 'let us go into the dining-room, it is there only that I can see you.' They entered there; I shut the door of it, which was of glass. The King sat down, the Queen on his left hand, Madame Elizabeth on his right, Madame Royale almost in front; the young Prince remained standing between his Father's legs. They all leaned towards him, and often held him embraced. This scene of woe lasted an hour and three-quarters; during which we could hear nothing; we could see only that always when the King spoke, the sobbings of the Princesses redoubled, continued for some minutes; and that then the King began again to speak.'—And so our meetings and our partings do now end! The sorrows we gave each other; the poor joys we faithfully shared, and all our lovings and our sufferings, and confused toilings under the earthly Sun, are over. Thou good soul, I shall never, never through all ages of Time, see thee any more!— NEVER! O Reader, knowest thou that hard word?

"For nearly two hours this agony lasts; then they tear themselves asunder. 'Promise that you will see us on the morrow.' He promises:—Ah yes, yes; yet once; and go now, ye loved ones; cry to God for yourselves and me!—It was a hard scene, but it is over. He will not see them on the morrow. The Queen, in passing through the ante-room, glanced at the Cerberus Municipals; and, with woman's vehemence, said through her tears, '*Vous êtes tous des scélérats.*'

"King Louis slept sound, till five in the morning, when Cléry, as he had been ordered, awoke him.

Cléry dressed his hair: while this went forward, Louis took a ring from his watch, and kept trying it on his finger; it was his wedding-ring, which he is now to return to the Queen as a mute farewell. At half-past six, he took the Sacrament; and continued in devotion, and conference with Abbé Edgeworth. He will not see his Family: it were too hard to bear.

"At eight, the Municipals enter: the King gives them his Will, and messages and effects; which they, at first, brutally refuse to take charge of: he gives them a roll of gold pieces, a hundred and twenty-five louis; these are to be returned to Malesherbes, who had lent them. At nine, Santerre says the hour is come. The King begs yet to retire for three minutes. At the end of three minutes, Santerre again says the hour is come. 'Stamping on the ground with his right-foot, Louis answers: " *Partons,* Let us go." '—How the rolling of those drums comes in, through the Temple bastions and bulwarks, on the heart of a queenly wife; soon to be a widow! He is gone, then, and has not seen us? A Queen weeps bitterly; a King's Sister and Children. Over all these Four does Death also hover: all shall perish miserably save one; she, as Duchesse d'Angoulême, will live,—not happily.

"At the Temple Gate were some faint cries, perhaps from voices of pitiful women: *'Grace! Grace!'* Through the rest of the streets there is silence as of the grave. No man not armed is allowed to be there: the armed, did any even pity, dare not express it, each man overawed by all his neighbours. All windows are down, none seen looking through them. All shops are shut. No wheel-carriage rolls, this morning, in these streets but one only. Eighty-thousand armed men stand ranked, like armed statues of men; cannons bristle, cannoneers with match burning, but no word or movement: it is as a city enchanted into silence and stone; one carriage with its escort, slowly rumbling, is the only sound. Louis reads, in his Book of Devotion, the Prayers of the Dying: clatter of this death-march falls sharp on the ear, in the great silence, but the thought would fain struggle heavenward, and forget the Earth.

"As the clocks strike ten, behold the Place de la Révolution, once Place de Louis Quinze: the Guillotine, mounted near the old Pedestal where once stood the Statue of that Louis! Far round, all bristles with cannons and armed men: spectators crowding in the rear; D'Orleans Egalité there in cabriolet.

Swift messengers, *hoquetons,* speed to the Townhall, every three minutes: near by is the Convention sitting,—vengeful for Lepelletier.   Heedless of all, Louis reads his Prayers of the Dying; not till five minutes yet has he finished; then the Carriage opens. What temper he is in?   Ten different witnesses will give ten different accounts of it.   He is in the collision of all tempers; arrived now at the black Mahlstrom and descent of Death: in sorrow, in indignation, in resignation struggling to be resigned.   'Take care of M. Edgeworth,' he straitly charges the Lieutenant who is sitting with them: then they two descend.

"The drums are beating: '*Taisez-vous,* Silence!' he cries 'in a terrible voice, *d'une voix terrible.*'   He mounts the scaffold, not without delay; he is in puce coat, breeches of gray, white stockings.   He strips off the coat; stands disclosed in a sleeve-waistcoat of white flannel.   The Executioners approach to bind him: he spurns, resists; Abbé Edgeworth has to remind him how the Saviour, in whom men trust, submitted to be bound.   His hands are tied, his head bare; the fatal moment is come.   He advances to the edge of the Scaffold, 'his face very red,' and says: 'Frenchmen, I die innocent: it is from this

Scaffold and near appearing before God that I tell you so. I pardon my enemies; I desire that France——' A General on horseback, Santerre or another, prances out, with uplifted hand: '*Tambours!*' The drums drown the voice. 'Executioners, do your duty!' The Executioners, desperate lest themselves be murdered (for Santerre and his Armed Ranks will strike, if they do not), seize the hapless Louis: six of them desperate, him singly desperate, struggling there; and bind him to their plank. Abbé Edgeworth, stooping, bespeaks him: 'Son of Saint Louis, ascend to Heaven.' The Axe clanks down; a King's Life is shorn away. It is Monday the 21st of January, 1793. He was aged Thirty-eight years four months and twenty-eight days.

"Executioner Samson shows the Head; fierce shout of *Vive la Republique* rises, and swells; caps raised on bayonets, hats waving: students of the College of Four Nations take it up, on the far Quais; fling it over Paris. D'Orleans drives off in his cabriolet: the Townhall Councillors rub their hands, saying, 'It is done, It is done.' There is dipping of handkerchiefs, of pike-points in the blood. Headsman Samson, though he afterwards denied it, sells locks

of the hair: fractions of the puce coat are long after
worn in rings.—And so, in some half-hour it is
done; and the multitude has all departed. Pastry-
cooks, coffee-sellers, milkmen sing out their trivial
quotidian cries: the world wags on, as if this were
a common day. In the coffeehouses that evening,
says Prudhomme, Patriot shook hands with Patriot
in a more cordial manner than usual. Not till some
days after, according to Mercier, did public men
see what a grave thing it was."

Charlotte Corday

"Amid which dim ferment of Caen and the World,
History specially notices one thing: in the lobby of
the Mansion *de l'Intendance,* where busy Deputies
are coming and going, a young Lady with an aged
valet, taking grave graceful leave of Deputy Barbaroux. She is of stately Norman figure; in her
twenty-fifth year; of beautiful still countenance: her
name is Charlotte Corday, heretofore styled D'Ar-
mans, while Nobility still was. Barbaroux has given
her a Note to Deputy Duperret,—him who once
drew his sword in the effervescence. Apparently
she will to Paris on some errand? 'She was a Republican before the Revolution, and never wanted

energy.' A completeness, a decision is in this fair female Figure: 'by energy she means the spirit that will prompt one to sacrifice himself for his country.' What if she, this fair young Charlotte, had emerged from her secluded stillness, suddenly like a Star; cruel-lovely, with half-angelic, half-dæmonic splendour; to gleam for a moment, and in a moment be extinguished: to be held in memory, so bright complete was she, through long centuries!—Quitting Cimmerian Coalitions without, and the dim-simmering Twenty-five millions within, History will look fixedly at this one fair Apparition of a Charlotte Corday; will note whither Charlotte moves, how the little Life burns forth so radiant, then vanishes swallowed of the Night.

"With Barbaroux's Note of Introduction, and slight stock of luggage, we see Charlotte on Tuesday the ninth of July seated in the Caen Diligence, with a place for Paris. None takes farewell of her, wishes her Good-journey: her Father will find a line left, signifying that she is gone to England, that he must pardon her, and forget her. The drowsy Diligence lumbers along; amid drowsy talk of Politics, and praise of the Mountain; in which she mingles not: all night, all day, and again all night. On

Thursday, not long before noon, we are at the bridge of Neuilly; here is Paris with her thousand black domes, the goal and purpose of thy journey! Arrived at the Inn de la Providence in the Rue des Vieux Augustins, Charlotte demands a room; hastens to bed; sleeps all afternoon and night, till the morrow morning.

"On the morrow morning, she delivers her Note to Duperret. It relates to certain Family Papers which are in the Minister of the Interior's hand; which a Nun at Caen, an old Convent-friend of Charlotte's, has need of; which Duperret shall assist her in getting: this then was Charlotte's errand to Paris? She has finished this, in the course of Friday;—yet says nothing of returning. She has seen and silently investigated several things. The Convention, in bodily reality, she has seen; what the Mountain is like. The living physiognomy of Marat she could not see; he is sick at present, and confined to home.

"About eight on the Saturday morning, she purchases a large sheath-knife in the Palais Royal; then straightway, in the Place des Victoires, takes a hackney-coach: 'To the Rue de l'Ecole de Médecine, No. 44.' It is the residence of the Citoyen Marat!

—The Citoyen Marat is ill, and can not be seen; which seems to disappoint her much. Her business is with Marat, then? Hapless beautiful Charlotte; hapless squalid Marat! From Caen in the utmost West, from Neuchâtel in the utmost East, they two are drawing nigh each other; they two have, very strangely, business together.—Charlotte, returning to her Inn, despatches a short Note to Marat; signifying that she is from Caen, the seat of rebellion; that she desires earnestly to see him, and 'will put it in his power to do France a great service.' No answer. Charlotte writes another Note, still more pressing; sets out with it by coach, about seven in the evening, herself. Tired day-labourers have again finished their Week; huge Paris is circling and simmering, manifold, according to its vague wont: this one fair Figure has decision in it; drives straight,—towards a purpose.

"It is yellow July evening, we say, the thirteenth of the month: eve of the Bastille day,—when 'M. Marat,' four years ago, in the crowd of the Pont Neuf, shrewdly required of that Besenval Hussar-party, which had such friendly dispositions, 'to dismount, and give up their arms, then;' and became notable among Patriot men. Four years: what a road he has travelled;—and sits now, about half-past seven of the clock, stewing in slipper-bath; sore afflicted; ill of Revolution Fever,—of what other malady this History had rather not name.   Excessively sick and worn, poor man: with precisely eleven-pence-halfpenny of ready money, in paper; with slipper-bath; strong three-footed stool for writing on, the while; and a squalid—Washerwoman, one may call her: that is his civic establishment in Medical-School Street; thither and not elsewhither has his road led him.   Not to the reign of Brotherhood and Perfect Felicity; yet surely on the way towards that?—Hark, a rap again!   A musical woman's voice, refusing to be rejected: it is the Citoyenne who would do France a service.   Marat, recognising from within, cries, Admit her.   Charlotte Corday is admitted.

"Citoyen Marat, I am from Caen the seat of rebellion, and wished to speak with you.—Be seated, *mon enfant*.   Now what are the Traitors doing at Caen?   What Deputies are at Caen?—Charlotte names some Deputies.   'Their heads shall fall within a fortnight,' croaks the eager People's-friend, clutching his tablets to write: *Barbaroux, Petion,* writes he with bare shrunk arm, turning aside in the bath:

Petion, and *Louvet,* and—Charlotte has drawn her
knife from the sheath; plunges it, with one sure
stroke, into the writer's heart. '*A moi, chère amie,*
Help, dear!' no more could the Death-choked say or
shriek. The helpful Washerwoman running in,
there is no Friend of the People, or Friend of the
Washerwoman left; but his life with a groan
gushes out, indignant, to the shades below.

"And so Marat People's-friend is ended; the
lone Stylites has got hurled down suddenly from
his Pillar—*whitherward* He that made him knows.
Patriot Paris may sound triple and tenfold, in dole
and wail; re-echoed by Patriot France; and the Convention, 'Chabot pale with terror, declaring that
they are to be all assassinated,' may decree him Pan-
theon Honours, Public Funeral, Mirabeau's dust
making way for him; and Jacobin Societies, in la-
mentable oratory, summing up his character, paral-
lel him to One, whom they think it honour to call
'the good Sansculotte,'—whom we name not here;
also a Chapel may be made, for the urn that holds
his Heart, in the Place du Carrousel; and new-born
children be named Marat; and Lago-di-Como
Hawkers bake mountains of stucco into unbeautiful

Busts; and David paint his Picture, or Death-Scene; and such other Apotheosis take place as the human genius, in these circumstances, can devise: but Marat returns no more to the light of this Sun. One sole circumstance we have read with clear sympathy, in the old *Moniteur* Newspaper: how Marat's Brother comes from Neuchâtel to ask of the Convention, 'that the deceased Jean-Paul Marat's musket be given him.' For Marat too had a brother, and natural affections; and was wrapt once in swaddling-clothes, and slept safe in a cradle like the rest of us. Ye children of men!—a sister of his, they say, lives still to this day in Paris.

"As for Charlotte Corday, her work is accomplished; the recompense of it is near and sure. The *chère amie,* and neighbours of the house, flying at her, she 'overturns some movables,' entrenches herself till the gendarmes arrive; then quietly surrenders; goes quietly to the Abbaye Prison: she alone quiet, all Paris sounding, in wonder, in rage or admiration, round her. Duperret is put in arrest, on account of her; his Papers sealed,—which may lead to consequences. Fauchet, in like manner; though Fauchet had not so much as heard of her. Charlotte,

confronted with these two Deputies, praises the
grave firmness of Duperret, censures the dejection
of Fauchet.

"On Wednesday morning, the thronged Palais
de Justice and Revolutionary Tribunal can see her
face; beautiful and calm: she dates it 'fourth day
of the Preparation of Peace.' A strange murmur
ran through the Hall, at sight of her; you could not
say of what character. Tinville has his indictments
and tape-papers: the cutler of the Palais Royal will
testify that he sold her the sheath-knife; 'All these
details are needless,' interrupted Charlotte; 'it is I
that killed Marat.' By whose instigation?—'By no
one's.' What tempted you, then? His crimes. 'I
killed one man,' added she, raising her voice extremely (*extrêmement*), as they went on with their
questions, 'I killed one man to save a hundred thousand; a villain to save innocents; a savage wild-
beast to give repose to my country. I was a Republican before the Revolution; I never wanted energy.'
There is therefore nothing to be said. The public
gazes astonished: the hasty limners sketch her
features, Charlotte not disapproving: the men of law
proceed with their formalities. The doom is Death
as a murderess. To her Advocate she gives thanks;

in gentle phrase, in high-flown classical spirit. To
the Priest they send her she gives thanks; but needs
not any shriving, any ghostly or other aid from him.

"On this same evening therefore, about half-past
seven o'clock, from the gate of the Conciergerie, to
a City all on tiptoe, the fatal Cart issues; seated on
it a fair young creature, sheeted in red smock of
Murderess; so beautiful, serene, so full of life; jour-
neying towards death,—alone amid the World.
Many take off their hats, saluting reverently; for
what heart but must be touched? Others growl and
howl. Adam Lux, of Mentz, declares that she is
greater than Brutus; that it were beautiful to die
with her: the head of this young man seems turned.
At the Place de la Révolution, the countenance of
Charlotte wears the same still smile. The executioners proceed to bind her feet; she resists, thinking it meant as an insult; on a word of explanation,
she submits with cheerful apology. As the last act,
all being now ready, they take the neckerchief from
her neck; a blush of maidenly shame overspreads
that fair face and neck; the cheeks were still tinged
with it when the executioner lifted the severed head,
to show it to the people. 'It is most true,' says Forster, 'that he struck the cheek insultingly; for I saw

it with my eyes: the Police imprisoned him for it.'

"In this manner have the Beautifullest and the Squalidest come in collision, and extinguished one another. Jean-Paul Marat and Marie-Anne Charlotte Corday both, suddenly, are no more. 'Day of the Preparation of Peace?' Alas, how were peace possible or preparable, while, for example, the hearts of lovely Maidens, in their convent-stillness, are dreaming not of Love-paradises, and the light of Life; but of Codrus'-sacrifices, and Death well-earned? That Twenty-five million hearts have got to such temper, this *is* the Anarchy; the soul of it lies in this: whereof not peace can be the embodiment! The death of Marat, whetting old animosities tenfold, will be worse than any life. O ye hapless Two, mutually extinctive, the Beautiful and the Squalid, sleep ye well,—in the Mother's bosom that bore you both!

"This is the History of Charlotte Corday; most definite, most complete; angelic-dæmonic: like a Star!"

The Whiff of Grape-Shot

"The Convention, driven such a course by wild wind, wild tide and steerage and non-steerage, these three years, has become weary of its own existence, sees all men weary of it; and wishes heartily to finish. To the last, it has to strive with contradictions: it is now getting fast ready with a Constitution, yet knows no peace. Sieyes, we say, is making the Constitution once more; has as good as made it. Warned by experience, the great Architect alters much, admits much. Distinction of Active and Passive Citizen that is, Money-qualification for Electors: nay Two Chambers, 'Council of Ancients,' as well as 'Council of Five-hundred;' to that conclusion have we come! In a like spirit, eschewing that fatal self-denying ordinance of your Old Constituents, we enact not only that actual Convention Members are re-eligible, but that Two-thirds of them must be re-elected. The Active Citizen Electors shall for this time have free choice of only One-third of their National Assembly. Such enactment, of Two-thirds to be re-elected, we append to our Constitution; we submit our Constitution to the Townships of France, and say, Accept *both,* or reject both. Unsavoury as this appendix may be, the Townships, by overwhelming majority, accept and ratify. With Directory of Five: with Two good Chambers, double-majority of them nominated by ourselves, one hopes this Constitution may prove final. *March* it will; for the legs of it, the re-elected Two-thirds, are already here, able to march. Sieyes looks at his paper-fabric with just pride.

"But now see how the contumacious Sections, Lepelletier foremost, kick against the pricks! Is it not manifest infraction of one's Elective Franchise, Rights of Man, and Sovereignty of the People, this appendix of re-electing *your* Two-thirds? Greedy tyrants who would perpetuate yourselves!—For the truth is, victory over Saint-Antoine, and long right of Insurrection, has spoiled these men. Nay spoiled all men. Consider too how each man was free to hope what he liked; and now there is to be no hope, there is to be fruition, fruition of *this*. . . .

"The convention has some Five-thousand regular troops at hand; Generals in abundance; and a Fifteen-hundred of miscellaneous persecuted Ultra-Jacobins, whom in this crisis it has hastily got together and armed, under the title *Patriots of Eighty-nine*. Strong in Law, it sends its General Menou to disarm Lepelletier.

"General Menou marches accordingly, with due summons and demonstration; with no result. Gen-

eral Menou, about eight in the evening, finds that he
is standing ranked in the Rue Vivienne, emitting
vain summonses; with primed guns pointed out of
every window at him; and that he can not disarm
Lepelletier. He has to return, with whole skin, but
without success; and be thrown into arrest, as 'a
traitor.' Whereupon the whole Forty-thousand join
this Lepelletier which can not be vanquished: to
what hand shall a quaking Convention now turn?
Our poor Convention, after such voyaging, just entering harbour, so to speak, has *struck on the bar;*—
and labours there frightfully, with breakers roaring
round it, Forty-thousand of them, like to wash it,
and its Sieyes Cargo and the whole future of France,
into the deep! Yet one last time, it struggles, ready
to perish.

"Some call for Barras to be made Commandant;
he conquered in Thermidor. Some, what is more
to the purpose, bethink them of the Citizen Buonaparte, unemployed Artillery-Officer, who took Tou-
lon. A man of head, a man of action: Barras is
named Commandant's-Cloak; this young Artillery-
Officer is named Commandant. He was in the Gallery at the moment, and heard it : he withdrew, some

half-hour, to consider with himself: after a half-hour of grim compressed considering, to be or not to be, he answers *Yea*.

"And now, a man of head being at the centre of it, the whole matter gets vital. Swift, to Camp of Sablons; to secure the Artillery, there are not twenty men guarding it! A swift Adjutant, Murat is the name of him, gallops; gets thither some minutes within time, for Lepelletier was also on march that way: the Cannon are ours. And now beset this post, and beset that; rapid and firm: at Wicket of the Louvre, in Cul-de-sac Dauphin, in Rue Saint-Honoré, from Pont-Neuf all along the north Quays southward to Pont *ci-devant* Royal,—rank round the Sanctuary of the Tuileries, a ring of steel discipline; let every gunner have his match burning, and all men stand to their arms!

"Thus there is Permanent-session through the night; and thus at sunrise of the morrow, there is seen sacred Insurrection once again: vessel of State labouring on the bar; and tumultuous sea all round her, beating *générale,* arming and sounding,—not ringing tocsin, for we have left no tocsin but our own in the Pavilion of Unity. It is an imminence of shipwreck, for the whole world to gaze at.

Frightfully she labours, that poor ship, within cable-length of port; huge peril for her. However, she has a man at the helm. Insurgent messages, received and not received; messenger admitted blindfolded; counsel and counter-counsel: the poor ship labours!—Vendémiaire 13th, year 4: curious enough, of all days, it is the Fifth day of October, anniversary of that Menad-march, six years ago; by sacred right of Insurrection wc are got thus far.

"Lepelletier has seized the Church of Saint-Roch; has seized the Pont-Ncuf, our piquet there retreating without fire. Stray shots fall from Lepelletier; rattle down on the very Tuileries Staircase. On the other hand, women advance dishevelled, shrieking, Peace; Lepelletier behind them waving its hat in sign that we shall fraternise. Steady! The Artillery-Officer is steady as bronze; can, if need were, be quick as lightning. He sends eight-hundred muskets with ball-cartridges to the Convention itself; honourable Members shall act with these in case of extremity: whereat they look grave enough. Four of the afternoon is struck. Lepelletier, making nothing by messengers, by fraternity or hat-waving, bursts out, along the Southern Quai Voltaire, along streets and passages, treble-quick in huge veritable onslaught! Whereupon, thou bronze Artillery-Officer—? 'Fire!' say the bronze lips. And roar and thunder, roar and again roar, continual, volcano-like, goes his great gun, in the Cul-de-sac Dauphin against the Church of Saint-Roch; go his great guns on the Pont-Royal; go all his great guns;—blow to air some two-hundred men, mainly about the Church of Saint-Roch! Lepelletier can not stand such horse-play; no Sectioner can stand it; the Forty-thousand yield on all sides, scour towards covert. 'Some hundred or so of them, gathered about the Théâtre de la République; but,' says he, 'a few shells dislodged them. It was all finished at six.'

"The Ship is *over* the bar, then; free she bounds shoreward,—amid shouting and vivats! Citoyen Buonaparte is 'named General of the Interior, by acclamation;' quelled Sections have to disarm in such humour as they may; sacred right of Insurrection is gone forever! The Sieyes Constitution can disembark itself, and begin marching. The miraculous Convention Ship has got to land;—and is there, shall we figuratively say, changed, as Epic Ships are wont, into a kind of *Sea Nymph,* never to sail more; to roam the waste Azure, a Miracle in History!

" 'It is false,' says Napoleon, 'that we fired first

with blank charge; it had been a waste of life to do that.' Most false: the firing was with sharp and sharpest shot: to all men it was plain that here was no sport; the rabbets and plinths of Saint-Roch Church show splintered by it to this hour.—Singular: in old Broglie's time, six years ago, this Whiff of Grapeshot was promised; but it could not be given then; could not have profited then. Now, however, the time is come for it, and the man; and behold, you have it; and the thing we specifically call *French Revolution* is blown into space by it, and become a thing that was!—"

CHAPTER XII

AN adequate discussion of Carlyle's relation to English Radicalism is impossible here, but no reader of Carlyle should overlook the striking pamphlet, written in 1839 and published in 1840, in which the historian of the French Revolution attempted to point out what was wrong with the England of his own day. As early as 1819 Carlyle had betrayed strong social sympathy with the Radical position; later he had hoped to be editor of the Radical *London Review* (afterward the *London and Westminster*) which was controlled toward the end of its career by John Stuart Mill. But Carlyle, who was neither Whig nor Tory, and apparently never cast a ballot in his life, found it impossible to work in harmony with political Radicalism. He attended two or three Radical meetings, early in his London life, but without giving his intellectual assent; and there was an indestructible "respectability" in this

Scotchman which made him rebel against the personal character of many Radical leaders. "Radical houses," he reports in one of his letters, "are little hells of improvidence, discord and unreason."

The point to be emphasized is Carlyle's burning sympathy with the poor. His distrust of contemporary Literary Philosophical and Parliamentary Radicalism served but to intensify his feeling that the poor were without a helper. He saw that the problem of poverty lay deeper than any mere measure of political reform. "Chartism," he declares, "means the bitter discontent grown fierce and mad, the wrong condition therefore or the wrong disposition of the Working Classes of England." It is no wonder that Lockhart declined the article for the *Quarterly Review*, and that Mill, not yet estranged from Carlyle, wished to print it in his final number of the *Westminster Review*. But Carlyle, as we have said, preferred to print *Chartism* himself.

The Reform Bill of 1832, it must be remembered, had increased the dominance of the middle classes at the political expense of the lower classes. The Poor Law of 1834 was harsh in its measures and was hated by the working people. The program of the Chartists, therefore, called for universal manhood suffrage, annual parliaments, vote by ballot without property qualifications, the payment of members of Parliament, and equalized political districts. These "points" of Chartism had long been commonplaces of the parliamentary Radicals, but they were now supported, under eloquent popular leadership, by vast bodies of working men, determined to win their contentions by demonstrations of physical force. The climax did not come, in fact, until the gigantic fiasco of 1848, described in Kingsley's *Alton Locke;* but the moral situation was clear enough by 1839.

Carlyle's chief contribution to this long agitation was in furnishing what we should now call the "sociological" point of view. "Where the great mass of men is tolerably right, all is right; where they are not right, all is wrong."

Here is an epoch-making passage:

"What constitutes the well-being of a man? Many things; of which the wages he gets, and the bread he buys with them are but one preliminary item. Grant, however, that the wages were the whole; that once knowing the wages and the price of bread, we know all; then what are the wages? Statistic Inquiry, in its present unguided condition, can not tell. The average rate of day's wages is not correctly ascertained for any portion of this country; not only not for half-centuries, it is not even ascertained anywhere for decades or years: far from instituting comparisons with the past, the present itself is unknown to us. And then, given the average of wages, what is the constancy of employment; what is the difficulty of finding employment; the fluctuation from season to season, from year to year? Is it constant, calculable wages; or fluctuating, incalculable, more or less of the nature of gambling? This secondary circumstance, of quality in wages, is perhaps even more important than the primary one of quantity. Farther we ask, Can the labourer, by thrift and industry, hope to rise to mastership; or is such hope cut off from him? How is he related to his employer; by bonds of friendliness and mutual help; or by hostility, opposition, and chains of mutual necessity alone? In a word, what degree of contentment can a human creature be supposed to enjoy in that position? With hunger preying on him, his contentment is likely to be small! But even with abundance, his discontent, his real misery may be great. The labourer's feelings, his notion of being justly dealt with or unjustly; his wholesome composure, frugality, prosperity in the one case, his acrid unrest, recklessness, gin-drinking, and gradual ruin in the other,—how shall figures of arithmetic represent all this? So much is still to be ascertained; much of it by no means easy to ascertain! Till, among the 'Hill Cooly' and 'Dog-cart' questions, there arise in Parliament and extensively out of it a 'Condition-of-England question,' and quite a new set of inquirers and methods, little of it is likely to be ascertained.

"One fact on this subject, a fact which arithmetic *is* capable of representing, we have often considered would be worth all the rest: Whether the labourer, whatever his wages are, is saving money? Laying up money, he proves that his condition, painful as it may be without and within, is not yet desperate; that he looks forward to a better day coming, and is still resolutely steering towards the same; that all the lights and darknesses of his lot are united under a blessed radiance of hope,—the last, first, nay one may say the sole blessedness of man. Is the habit of saving increased or increasing, or the contrary?"

Carlyle combats, of course, the *laissez faire* or "let alone" doctrine of the orthodox political economists. To him it is "false, heretical, and damnable."

The lower classes must be taken care of by the higher; there must be supervision by a central authority; the laborer has a right to "that guidance and government which he can not give himself." Here is the central point of Carlyle's position,—and the point, of course, where he parts company with Mill and the whole trend of modern democracy. Carlyle hears from the multitude the inarticulate prayer: "Guide me, govern me! I am mad and miserable, and can not guide myself!" "Surely," he goes on, "of all 'rights of man,' this right of the ignorant man to be guided by the wiser, to be gently or forcibly held in the true course by him, is the indisputablest."

Then follows the indictment of Democracy, which the present-day reader will do well to compare with Lowell's address on Democracy, and with any of Abraham Lincoln's speeches:—

"Democracy, we are well aware, what is called 'self-government' of the multitude by the multitude, is in words everywhere passionately clamoured for at present. Democracy makes rapid progress in these latter times, and ever more rapid, in a perilous accelerative ratio; towards democracy, and that only, the progress of things is everywhere tending as to

the final goal and winning-post. So think, so
clamour the multitudes everywhere. And yet all
men may see, whose sight is good for much, that in
democracy can lie no finality; that with the com-
pletest winning of democracy there is nothing yet
won,—except emptiness, and the free chance to win!
Democracy is, by the nature of it, a self-cancelling
business; and gives in the long run a net result of
zero. Where no government is wanted, save that of
the parish-constable, as in America with its boundless soil, every man being able to find work and
recompense for himself, democracy may subsist; not
elsewhere, except briefly, as a swift transition toward something other and farther. Democracy
never yet, that we heard of, was able to accomplish
much work, beyond that same cancelling of itself.
Rome and Athens are themes for the schools; unex-
ceptionable for that purpose. In Rome and Athens
as elsewhere, if we look practically, we shall find
that it was not by loud voting and debating of many,
but by wise insight and ordering of a few that the
work was done. So it is ever, so will it ever be.
. . . Not towards the impossibility, 'self-government' of a multitude by a multitude; but towards

some possibility, government by the wisest, does bewildered Europe struggle."

The case for Democracy against Thomas Carlyle scarcely needs to be stated here. Mazzini stated it long ago when he affirmed that Carlyle believed in God and in the individual man, but not in the Collective Will. Most Americans and most Englishmen now believe that political wisdom is not the exclusive possession of any class, and that democratic government is increasingly justifying itself by training and choosing men who can solve the essential governmental problems. In no self-governing country of the world is there now discoverable, at any rate, a group of citizens whose prayer to the strong is: "Guide me, govern me! I am mad and miserable, and can not guide myself!"

Contemporary prayers to the strong are phrased somewhat differently from that!

CHAPTER XIII

HEROES AND HERO-WORSHIP

THE theory concerning the Strong Person, plainly hinted in *Chartism,* became the theme of Carlyle's next book: the lectures, namely, on *Heroes, Hero-Worship and the Heroic in History,* which were delivered to fashionable London audiences in 1840 and were published in 1841. They were his fourth-and-last-course of lectures, and the only ones that have been preserved. It was Carlyle's custom to "splash down" on paper the things that he was likely to wish to say in public; but he usually spoke without notes, and with great rapidity, "like wild Annandale grape-shot." The physical and mental ordeal of public speaking was a serious matter for a man of Carlyle's temperament, and he abandoned this "mixture of prophecy and play-acting" as soon as the income from his books made it no longer necessary. Professor MacMechan, who edited *Heroes* with the same definitive scholarship which he had previously devoted to *Sartor,* gives a most interesting account of Carlyle's manner of delivery and of the various moods in which Londoners of 1840 listened to the lectures. It must be remembered that the material now before us in *Heroes* was entirely rewritten, after the lectures were delivered, although the characteristics of oral style are even more sharply marked than is usual in Carlyle's writing.

The germinal idea of the six lectures is in a sentence of Hume: "The same principles naturally deify mortals superior in power, courage, or understanding, and produce hero-worship." But in Carlyle's eyes, the "super-man" is not so much the product of a surplusage of force—in Nietzsche's sense of the word—as of "sincerity." Now sincerity, according to Carlyle, implies superior insight into truth and loyalty to it. Not the logical processes of the "Understanding," but the mystical perceptions of the "Reason," constitute the "hero's" superiority to other men, and establish his claim to true leadership among men. Thus our loyalty to the "hero" is in reality a loyalty to Truth itself,—that Truth first mystically perceived by the Hero,—and "this loyalty of all men to great men is a mystic bond. For loyalty to the Hero is loyalty to the Eternal—it is more, it is acquiescence in the divine plan."

I quote these last words from an unpublished essay by Mr. B. H. Lehman, who has likewise an acute comment upon what he terms "the mutability of the hero-stuff,"—in other words that Carlylese theory of the "interchangeable" or "standardized" Hero which has puzzled so many readers: "All sorts of Heroes have a common source of truth. The form of any particular Hero depends upon his course of life and education—his environment. Thus the pressure and the need of a world of men diversify the forms which the essential Hero assumes. The definite elements of the Hero Theory are accordingly these: a Hero, characterized by *sincerity,* which is truth of insight and veracity of conduct; a world of men characterized by reverence for the Hero and by need of him; and, resulting from the interplay of the great-man and the world of men, the Protean attitude of the Hero."

In the light of this analysis, it is easy to see why Carlyle could utilize, in support of his main contention, such an odd collection of "super-men" as Odin, Mahomet, Dante, Shakespeare, Luther, Knox, Johnson, Rousseau, Burns, Cromwell and Napoleon. All of these persons, surely, possessed some superior "insight," and therefore become to us revealers of the Divine Fact. The qualities which mark such *Heroes* are precisely the qualities which Carlyle had been praising for fifteen years in his *Essays,* in *Sartor,* in *The French Revolution,* and in *Chartism;* and which he was soon to glorify in *Cromwell* and in *Frederick.*

But let us listen to Carlyle himself. First, as to his theme :—

"We have undertaken to discourse here for a little on Great Men, their manner of appearance in our world's business, how they have shaped themselves in the world's history, what ideas men formed of them, what work they did;—on Heroes, namely, and on their reception and performance; what I call Hero-worship and the Heroic in human affairs. Too evidently this is a large topic; deserving quite other treatment than we can expect to give it at present. A large topic; indeed, an illimitable one; wide as Universal History itself. For, as I take it, Universal History, the history of what man has accomplished in this world, is at bottom the History of the Great Men who have worked here. They were the leaders of men, these great ones; the modellers, patterns, and in a wide sense creators, of whatsoever

the general mass of men contrived to do or to attain;
all things that we see standing accomplished in the
world are properly the outer material result, the
practical realization and embodiment, of Thoughts
that dwelt in the Great Men sent into the world:
the soul of the whole world's history, it may justly
be considered, were the history of these. Too clearly
it is a topic we shall do no justice to in this place!

"One comfort is, that Great Men, taken up in any
way, are profitable company. We can not look, however imperfectly, upon a great man, without gaining
something by him. He is the living light-fountain,
which it is good and pleasant to be near. The light
which enlightens, which has enlightened the darkness of the world; and this not as a kindled lamp
only, but rather as a natural luminary shining by
the gift of Heaven; a flowing light-fountain, as I
say, of native original insight, of manhood and heroic nobleness;—in whose radiance all souls feel that
it is well with them. On any terms whatsoever, you
will not grudge to wander in such neighbourhood
for a while. These Six classes of Heroes, chosen
out of widely distant countries and epochs, and in
mere external figure differing altogether, ought, if
we look faithfully at them, to illustrate several

things for us. Could we see *them* well, we should get some glimpses into the very marrow of the world's history. How happy, could I but, in any measure, in such times as these, make manifest to you the meanings of Heroism; the divine relation (for I may well call it such) which in all times unites a Great Man to other men; and thus, as it were, not exhaust my subject, but so much as break ground on it! At all events, I must make the attempt."

Next, note Carlyle's explanation of the Great Man's "Sincerity":—

"But of a Great Man especially, of him I will venture to assert that it is incredible he should have been other than true. It seems to me the primary foundation of him, and of all that can lie in him, this. No Mirabeau, Napoleon, Burns, Cromwell, no man adequate to do anything, but is first of all in right earnest about it; what I call a sincere man. I should say *sincerity*, a deep, great, genuine sincerity, is the first characteristic of all men in any way heroic. Not the sincerity that calls itself sincere; ah no, that is a very poor matter indeed;—a shallow braggart conscious sincerity; oftenest self-conceit mainly. The Great Man's sincerity is of the kind he can not speak of, is not conscious of: nay, I suppose, he is conscious rather of *in*sincerity; for what man can walk accurately by the law of truth for one day? No, the Great Man does not boast himself sincere, far from that; perhaps does not ask himself if he is so: I would say rather, his sincerity does not depend on himself; he can not help being sincere! The great Fact of Existence is great to him. Fly as he will, he can not get out of the awful presence of this Reality. His mind is so made; he is great by that, first of all. Fearful and wonderful, real as Life, real as Death, is this Universe to him. Though all men should forget its truth, and walk in a vain show, he can not. At all moments the Flame-image glares in upon him; undeniable, there, there! —I wish you to take this as my primary definition of a Great Man. A little man may have this, it is competent to all men that God has made: but a Great Man can not be without it.

"Such a man is what we call an *original* man; he comes to us at first-hand. A messenger he, sent from the Infinite Unknown with tidings to us. We may call him Poet, Prophet, God;—in one way or other, we all feel that the words he utters are as no other man's words. Direct from the Inner Fact of things;—he lives, and has to live, in daily communion with that. Hearsays can not hide it from him; he is blind, homeless, miserable, following hearsays; *it* glares in upon him. Really his utterances, are they not a kind of 'revelation';—what we must call such for want of some other name? It is from the heart of the world that he comes; he is portion of the primal reality of things. God has made many revelations: but this man too, has not God made him, the latest and newest of all? The 'inspiration of the Almighty giveth *him* understanding': we must listen before all to him."

Here are two brief passages dealing with the "mutability of the hero-stuff" :—

"For at bottom the Great Man, as he comes from the hand of Nature, is ever the same kind of thing: Odin, Luther, Johnson, Burns; I hope to make it appear that these are all originally of one stuff; that only by the world's reception of them, and the shapes they assume, are they so immeasurably diverse. The worship of Odin astonishes us,—to fall prostrate before the Great Man, into *deliquium* of love and wonder over him, and feel in their hearts that he was a denizen of the skies, a god! This was imperfect enough: but to welcome, for example, a Burns as we did, was that what we can call perfect?

The most precious gift that Heaven can give to the
Earth; a man of 'genius' as we call it; the Soul of
a Man actually sent down from the skies with a
God's-message to us,—this we waste away as an
idle artificial firework, sent to amuse us a little, and
sink it into ashes, wreck and ineffectuality: *such*
reception of a Great Man I do not call very perfect
either! Looking into the heart of the thing, one
may perhaps call that of Burns a still uglier phenomenon, betokening still sadder imperfections in mankind's ways, than the Scandinavian method itself!
To fall into mere unreasoning *deliquium* of love and
admiration, was not good; but such unreasoning,
nay irrational supercilious no-love at all is perhaps
still worse!—It is a thing forever changing, this of
Hero-worship: different in each age, difficult to do
well in any age. Indeed, the heart of the whole
business of the age, one may say, is to do it well."

"We have repeatedly endeavoured to explain that
all sorts of Heroes are intrinsically of the same material; that given a great soul, open to the Divine
Significance of Life, then there is given a man fit
to speak of this, to sing of this, to fight and work
for this, in a great, victorious, enduring manner;
there is given a Hero,—the outward shape of whom

will depend on the time and the environment he finds himself in. The Priest, too, as I understand it, is a kind of Prophet; in him too there is required to be a light of inspiration, as we must name it. He presides over the worship of the people; is the Uniter of them with the Unseen Holy. He is the Spiritual Captain of the people; as the Prophet is their spiritual King with many captains: he guides them heavenward, by wise guidance through this Earth and its work. The ideal of him is, that he too be what we can call a voice from the unseen Heaven; interpreting, even as the Prophet did, and in a more familiar manner unfolding the same to men. The unseen Heaven,—the 'open secret of the Universe;'—which so few have an eye for! He is the Prophet shorn of his more awful splendour; burning with mild equable radiance, as the enlightener of daily life. This, I say, is the ideal of the Priest. So in old times; so in these, and in all times."

We must choose a single paragraph from Carlyle's delineation of the supremacy of Shakespeare:—

"Of this Shakespeare of ours, perhaps the opinion one sometimes hears a little idolatrously expressed is, in fact, the right one; I think the best judgment not of this country only, but of Europe at large, is slowly pointing to the conclusion, that Shakespeare is the chief of all Poets hitherto; the greatest intellect who, in our recorded world, has left record of himself in the way of Literature. On the whole, I know not such a power of vision, such a faculty of thought, if we take all the characters of it, in any other man. Such a calmness of depth; placid joyous strength; all things imaged in that great soul of his so true and clear, as in a tranquil unfathomable sea! It has been said, that in the constructing of Shakespeare's Dramas there is, apart from all other 'faculties' as they are called, an understanding manifested, equal to that in Bacon's *Novum Organum*. That is true; and it is not a truth that strikes every one. It would become more apparent if we tried, any of us for himself, how, out of Shakespeare's dramatic materials, *we* could fashion such a result! The built house seems all so fit,—every way as it should be, as if it came there by its own law and the nature of things,—we forget the rude disorderly quarry it was shaped from. The very perfection of the house, as if Nature herself had made it, hides the builder's merit. Perfect, more

perfect than any other man, we may call Shakespeare
in this: he discerns, knows as by instinct, what condition he works under, what his materials are, what
his own force and its relation to them is. It is not
a transitory glance of insight that will suffice; it is
deliberate illumination of the whole matter; it is a
calmly *seeing* eye; a great intellect, in short. How
a man, of some wide thing that he has witnessed,
will construct a narrative, what kind of picture and
delineation he will give of it,—is the best measure
you could get of what intellect is in the man. Which
circumstance is vital and shall stand prominent;
which unessential, fit to be suppressed; where is the
true *beginning,* the true sequence and ending? To
find out this, you task the whole force of insight
that is in the man. He must *understand* the thing;
according to the depth of his understanding, will
the fitness of his answer be. You will try him so.
Does like join itself to like; does the spirit of method
stir in that confusion, so that its embroilment becomes order? Can the man say, *Fiat lux,* Let there
be light; and out of chaos make a world? Precisely
as there is *light* in himself, will he accomplish this."

Finally, let us take the famous definition of Kingship,—hopelessly wrong in its etymology, but perfectly indicative of Carlyle's mature (and many will think perverse) view of politics:—

"We come now to the last form of Heroism; that which we call Kingship. The Commander over Men; he to whose will our wills are to be subordinated, and loyally surrender themselves, and find their welfare in doing so, may be reckoned the most important of Great Men. He is practically the summary for us of *all* the various figures of Heroism; Priest, Teacher, whatsoever of earthly or of spiritual dignity we can fancy to reside in a man, embodies itself here, to *command* over us, to furnish us with constant practical teaching, to tell us for the day and hour what we are to *do*. He is called *Rex,* Regulator, *Roi:* our own name is still better; King, *Könning,* which means *Can*-ning, Able-man.

"Numerous considerations, pointing towards deep, questionable, and indeed unfathomable regions, present themselves here: on the most of which we must resolutely for the present forbear to speak at all. As Burke said that perhaps fair *Trial by Jury* was the soul of Government, and that all legislation, administration, parliamentary debating,

and the rest of it, went on, in 'order to bring twelve
impartial men into a jury-box;'—so, by much
stronger reason, may I say here, that the finding of
your *Ableman* and getting him invested with the
symbols of ability, with dignity, worship (*worth*-
ship), royalty, kinghood, or whatever we call it,
so that *he* may actually have room to guide according to his faculty of doing it,—is the business, well
or ill accomplished, of all social procedure whatsoever in this world! Hustings-speeches, Parliamentary motions, Reform Bills, French Revolutions, all
mean at heart this; or else nothing. Find in any
country the Ablest Man that exists there; raise *him*
to the supreme place, and loyally reverence him:
you have a perfect government for that country; no
ballot-box, parliamentary eloquence, voting, consti-
tution-building, or other machinery whatsoever can
improve it a whit. It is in the perfect state; an ideal
country. The Ablest Man; he means also the truest-
hearted, justest, the Noblest Man: what he *tells us
to do* must be precisely the wisest, fittest, that we
could anywhere or anyhow learn;—the thing which
it will in all ways behoove us, with right loyal thank-
fulness and nothing doubting, to do! Our *doing*
and life were then, so far as government could reg-

ulate it, well regulated; that were the ideal of constitutions."

The foregoing exposition of one of the best-known of Carlyle's books does no justice to the extraordinary brilliancy of his varied portrait painting, or to the historical acumen by means of which he restored the dimly-understood figures of Mahomet and Cromwell and made them thenceforth living human beings in the imagination of Englishmen. But nobody who has enough intellectual interest to read Carlyle at all is likely to leave *Heroes and Hero-Worship* unread.

CHAPTER XIV.

PAST AND PRESENT

IN the first weeks of 1843 Carlyle laid aside temporarily his preparatory reading for *Cromwell,* and wrote, with a speed and ease unusual for him, another tract for the times. "I hope," he wrote to his mother, "it will be a rather useful kind of book. It goes rather in a fiery strain about the present condition of men in general, and the strange pass they are coming to; and I calculate it may awaken here and there a slumbering blockhead to rub his eyes and consider what he is about in God's creation —a thing highly desirable at present. I found I could not go on with Cromwell, or with anything else, till I had disburdened my heart somewhat in regard to all that. The look of the world is really quite oppressive to me. Eleven thousand souls in Paisley alone living on three-halfpence a day, and the governors of the land all busy shooting partridges and passing corn-laws the while! It is a thing no man with a speaking tongue in his head is entitled to be silent about. My only difficulty is that I have far too *much* to say, and require great address in deciding how to say it."

His picture of the "Past" was drawn from a book he had just been reading: Joceline de Brakelonde's chronicle of the Abbey of St. Edmund's Bury, at the close of the twelfth century. Contrasted with this picture of order and peace was the England of 1843, "dying of inanition," the rich growing richer and the poor poorer, in their "liberty" to buy in the cheapest market and to sell in the dearest. "To whom," he asks, "is this wealth of England wealth? Who is it that it blesses; makes happier, wiser, beautifuler, in any way better?"

Yet *Past and Present* is by no means a despairing book. Carlyle's prose never chanted a clearer song of Justice, of Labor, and of ultimate Reward.

"The soul of the world is just. . . . In this God's-world, with its wild-whirling eddies and mad foam-oceans, where men and nations perish as if without law, and judgment for an unjust thing is sternly delayed, dost thou think that there is therefore no justice? It is what the fool hath said in his heart. It is what the wise, in all times, were wise because they denied, and knew forever not to be. I tell thee again, there is nothing else but justice. One strong thing I find here below: the just thing, the true thing. My friend, if thou hadst all the artillery of Woolwich trundling at thy back in support of an unjust thing; and infinite bonfires visibly waiting ahead of thee, to blaze centuries long for thy victory on behalf of it,—I would advise thee to call halt, to fling down thy baton, and say, 'In God's name, No!' Thy 'success'? Poor devil, what will thy success amount to? If the thing is unjust, thou hast not succeeded; no, not though bonfires blazed from North to South, and bells rang, and editors wrote leading-articles, and the just thing lay trampled out of sight, to all mortal eyes an abolished and annihilated thing. Success? In few years thou wilt be dead and dark,—all cold, eyeless, deaf; no blaze of bonfires, ding-dong of bells or leading-articles visible or audible to thee again at all forever: What kind of success is that! . . . Towards an eternal centre of right and nobleness, and of that only, is all this confusion tending. We already know whither it is all tending; what will have victory, what will have none! The Heaviest will reach the centre. The Heaviest, sinking through complex fluctuating media and vortices, has its deflections, its obstructions, nay at times its resiliences, its reboundings; whereupon some blockhead shall be heard jubilating, 'See, your Heaviest ascends!'—but at all moments it is moving centreward, fast as is convenient for it; sinking, sinking; and, by laws older than the World, old as the Maker's first Plan of the World, it has to arrive there."

"A fair day's-wages for a fair day's-work" Carlyle considers to be a just demand. It is the everlasting right of man. Even "Gurth the swineherd, born thrall of Cedric the Saxon, tended pigs in the wood and did get some parings of the pork." The thrall of an English manufacturer, in 1843, is not getting them; the gospel of "Enlightened Selfishness," preached by political economists, does not work. The one healing remedy is "Hero-Worship," or government by the wisest, but the precedent condition for such government is "being ourselves of heroic mind": "a whole world of Heroes, that is what we aim at! Thou and I, my friend, can, in the most flunky world, make, each of us, *one* nonflunky, one hero, if we like: that will be two heroes to begin with: Courage! even that is a whole world of heroes to end with."

After these admonitions, which mark a distinct advance over the "Hero-theory" as Carlyle had previously phrased it, comes the picture of the laborious twelfth century abbey, presided over by Abbot Samson,—"a personable man of seven-and-forty; stout-made, stands erect as a pillar; with bushy eyebrows, the eyes of him beaming into you in a really strange way; the face massive, grave, with 'a very eminent nose'; his head almost bald, its auburn remnants of hair, and the copious ruddy beard, getting slightly streaked with gray. This is Brother Samson; a man worth looking at."

True enough, but we can not pause here to look further at him or at the work which he wrought. We must turn with Carlyle to the modern worker and the new gospel of Labor.

"All work, even cotton-spinning, is noble"; that is the key-note of Book Third. Happiness is negligible. The true human wages are what Tennyson was soon to call "The wages of going on." "The only happiness a brave man ever troubled himself with asking much about was, happiness enough to

get his work done. Not 'I can't eat!' but 'I can't
work!' that was the burden of all wise complaining
among men. It is, after all, the one unhappiness of
a man. That he can not work; that he can not get
his destiny as a man fulfilled. Behold, the day
is passing swiftly over, our life is passing swiftly
over; and the night cometh, wherein no man can
work. The night once come, our happiness, our
unhappiness,—it is all abolished; vanished, clean
gone; a thing that has been: 'not of the slightest
consequence' whether we were happy as eupeptic
Curtis, as the fattest pig of Epicurus, or unhappy
as Job with potsherds, as musical Byron with
Giaours and sensibilities of the heart; as the unmusical Meat-jack with hard labour and rust! But
our work,—behold that is not abolished, that has not
vanished: our work, behold, it remains, or the want
of it remains;—for endless Times and Eternities,
remains; and that is now the sole question with us
forevermore! Brief brawling Day, with its noisy
phantasms, its poor paper-crowns tinsel-gilt, is gone;
and divine everlasting Night, with her star-diadems,
with her silences and her veracities, is come! What
hast thou done, and how? Happiness, unhappiness:
all that was but the *wages* thou hadst; thou hast

spent all that, in sustaining thyself hitherward; not a coin of it remains with thee, it is all spent, eaten: and now thy work, where is thy work? Swift, out with it; let us see thy work!"

But to get the right work done, "labour must become a seeing national giant, with a *soul* in the body of him, and take his place on the throne of things." A mere abolition of the Corn-Laws is but a temporary expedient. Listen to Carlyle's prophecy, which has been as singularly fulfilled as was Burke's prophecy in his *Reflections on the French Revolution* concerning the rise of a military despot fulfilled by the career of Napoleon: "Yes, were the Corn-Laws ended to-morrow, there is nothing yet ended; there is only room made for all manner of things beginning. The Corn-Laws gone, and Trade made free, it is as good as certain this paralysis of industry will pass away. We shall have another period of commercial enterprise, of victory and prosperity; during which, it is likely, much money will again be made, and all the people may, by the extant methods, still for a space of years, be kept alive and physically fed. The strangling band of Famine will be loosened from our necks; we shall have room again to breathe; time to bethink our-

selves, to repent and consider! A precious and
thrice-precious space of years; wherein to struggle
as for life in reforming our foul ways; in alleviat-
ing, instructing, regulating our people; seeking, as
for life, that something like spiritual food be imparted them, some real governance and guidance be
provided them! It will be a priceless time. For
our new period or paroxsym of commercial prosperity will and can, on the old methods of 'Competi-
tion and Devil take the hindmost,' prove but a
paroxysm: a new paroxysm,—likely enough, if we
do not use it better, to be our *last*. In this, of itself,
is no salvation. If our Trade in twenty years,
'flourishing' as never Trade flourished, could double
itself; yet then also, by the old Laissez-faire method,
our Population is doubled: we shall then be as we
are, only twice as many of us, twice and ten times
as unmanageable!"

What is needed, says Carlyle, is a new type of
leader,—very different from the successful British
manufacturer of the day, "the indomitable Plugson
of the respected Firm of Plugson, Hunks and Company, in St. Dolly Undershot." The blind Plugson
might really become a real Captain of Industry, did
he but know it! Then follow the eloquent chapters

on Labor and Reward, asserting once more the nobility and sacredness of work. These chapters have been like a trumpet-call to many an American who can not share Carlyle's views on politics. For this prophet of better days to come can not close his impassioned argument without a characteristic attack upon "liberty," as Mill and modern democracy have understood that term. "Gurth's brass collar did not gall him: Cedric *deserved* to be his master. The pigs were Cedric's, but Gurth too would get his parings of them. Gurth had the inexpressible satisfaction of feeling himself related indissolubly, though in a rude brass-collar way, to his fellow-mortals in this Earth. He had superiors, inferiors, equals.—Gurth is now 'emancipated' long since; has what we call 'Liberty.' Liberty, I am told, is a divine thing. Liberty when it becomes the 'Liberty to die by starvation' is not so divine! Liberty? The true liberty of a man, you would say, consisted in his finding out, or being forced to find out the right path, and to walk thereon. To learn, or to be taught, what work he actually was able for; and then by permission, persuasion, and even compulsion, to set about doing of the same! That is his true blessedness, honour, 'liberty' and maximum of well-being:

if liberty be not that, I for one have small care about liberty."

Carlyle's difficulty lay in his distrust of humanity: in his wavering faith in his own doctrine of creating a "world of heroes" by beginning with two. "The grand problem," he confesses, "yet remains to solve: that of finding government by your Real Superiors! *Alas, how shall we ever learn the solution of that, benighted, bewildered, sniffing, sneering, God-forgetting unfortunates as we are?*"

But meantime there are certain concrete things that may be done, and here Carlyle is a modern of the moderns. How he anticipates twentieth-century legislation in passages like this: "Again, are not Sanitary Regulations possible for a Legislature? The old Romans had their Ædiles; who would, I think, in direct contravention to supply-and-demand, have rigourously seen rammed up into total abolition many a foul cellar in our Southwarks, St. Gileses, and dark poison-lanes; saying sternly, 'Shall a Roman man dwell there?' The Legislature, at whatever cost of consequences, would have had to answer, 'God forbid!'—The Legislature, even as it now is, could order all dingy Manufacturing Towns to cease from their soot and darkness; to let in the blessed sunlight, the blue of Heaven, and become clear and clean; to burn their coal-smoke, namely, and make flame of it. Baths, free air, a wholesome temperature, ceilings twenty feet high, might be ordained, by Act of Parliament, in all establishments licensed as Mills. There are such Mills already extant;—honour to the builders of them! The Legislature can say to others: Go ye and do likewise; better if you can.

"Every toiling Manchester, its smoke and soot all burnt, ought it not, among so many world-wide conquests, to have a hundred acres or so of free greenfield, with trees on it, conquered, for its little children to disport in; for its all-conquering workers to take a breath of twilight air in? You would say so! A willing Legislature could say so with effect. A willing Legislature could say very many things! And to whatsoever 'vested interest,' or such like, stood up, gainsaying merely, 'I shall lose profits,'— the willing Legislature would answer, 'Yes, but my sons and daughters will gain health, and life, and a soul.'—'What is to become of our Cotton-trade?' cried certain Spinners, when the Factory Bill was proposed; 'What is to become of our invaluable Cotton-trade?' The Humanity of England answered steadfastly: 'Deliver me these rickety perishing souls of infants, and let your Cotton-trade take its chance. God Himself commands the one thing; not God especially the other thing. We can not have prosperous Cotton-trades at the expense of keeping the Devil a partner in them!' "

And how prophetic has his vision of profit-sharing become! "A question arises here: Whether, in some ulterior, perhaps not far-distant stage of this 'Chivalry of Labour,' your Master-Worker may not find it possible, and needful, to grant his Workers permanent *interest* in his enterprise and theirs? So that it become, in practical result, what in essential fact and justice it ever is, a joint enterprise; all men, from the Chief Master down to the lowest Overseer and Operative, economically as well as loyally concerned for it?—Which question I do not answer. The answer, near or else far, is perhaps, Yes;—and yet one knows the difficulties. Despotism is essential in most enterprises; I am told, they do not tolerate 'freedom of debate' on board a Seventy-four! Republican senate and *plebiscita* would not answer well in Cotton-Mills. And yet observe there too: Freedom, not nomad's or ape's Freedom, but man's Freedom; this is indispensable.

We must have it, and will have it! To reconcile
Despotism with Freedom:—well, is that such a mystery? Do you not already know the way? It is to
make your Despotism *just*. Rigourous as Destiny;
but just too, as Destiny and its Laws. The Laws
of God: all men obey these, and have no 'Freedom'
at all but in obeying them. The way is already
known, part of the way;—and courage and some
qualities are needed for walking on it!"

Finally, like the song of a Dante emerging from
Hell into the clear sweet upper air, comes Carlyle's
closing chant to the Workers:

"But it is to you, ye Workers, who do already
work, and are as grown men, noble and honourable
in a sort, that the whole world calls for new work
and nobleness. Subdue mutiny, discord, wide-
spread despair, by manfulness, justice, mercy and
wisdom. Chaos is dark, deep as Hell; let light be;
and there is instead a green flowery world. Oh, it
is great, and there is no other greatness. To make
some nook of God's Creation a little fruitfuler, better, more worthy of God; to make some human
hearts a little wiser, manfuler, happier—more
blessed, less accursed! It is work for a God. Sooty
Hell of Mutiny and savagery and despair can, by

man's energy, be made a kind of Heaven; cleared
of its soot, of its mutiny, of its need to mutiny; the
everlasting arch of Heaven's azure overspanning *it*
too, and its cunning mechanism and tall chimney-
steeples, as a birth of Heaven; God and all men
looking on it well pleased.

"Unstained by wasteful deformities, by wasted
tears or heart's-blood of men, or any defacement
of the Pit, noble fruitful Labour, growing ever
nobler, will come forth,—the grand sole miracle
of Man; whereby Man has risen from the low places
of this Earth, very literally, into divine Heavens.
Ploughers, Spinners, Builders; Prophets, Poets,
Kings; Brindleys and Goethes, Odins and Ark-
wrights; all martyrs, and noble men, and Gods are
of one grand Host; immeasurable; marching ever
forward since the beginnings of the World. The
enormous, all-conquering, flame-crowned Host, noble every soldier in it; sacred and alone noble. Let
him who is not of it hide himself; let him tremble
for himself. Stars at every button can not make
him noble; sheaves of Bath-garters, nor bushels of
Georges; nor any other contrivance but manfully
enlisting in it, valiantly taking place and step in it.
O Heavens will he not bethink himself; he too is so

needed in the Host! It were so blessed, thrice-
blessed, for himself and for us all! In hope of the
Last Partridge, and some Duke of Weimar among
our English Dukes, we will be patient yet a while.

> " 'The future hides in it
> Gladness and sorrow;
> We press still thorow,
> Nought that abides in it
> Daunting us,—onward.' "

CHAPTER XV.

OLIVER CROMWELL'S *Letters and Speeches with Elucidations,* published in 1845, is a work far different from Carlyle's original intentions. Twenty-three years before, he had planned an essay on the period of the Civil Wars and the Commonwealth, but it was never written. In December, 1838, Mill wished him to write on Cromwell for the *Westminster Review,* but Carlyle was forestalled by J. Robertson, the editor, who wanted the subject himself. Carlyle worked on Cromwell, nevertheless, throughout 1839, and in the lecture on *Cromwell as Hero* in 1840 he sketched the essential outline of his view of the Protector. To him, Oliver was an "Able-Man," an "inarticulate Captain,"—yet not so inarticulate as he seems. Carlyle accepted neither "the Tory myth of a regicide monster" nor "the Whig myth of a vulgar and ridiculous hypocrite," and even within the brief

200

limits of his Hero lecture he created a new Cromwell whom the world has come to accept as the real Cromwell. In 1843 Carlyle gave up his plan of writing a history of the whole period,—a task since then performed by S. R. Gardiner—and confined himself to annotations upon Cromwell's letters and speeches.

His instinct was wise. By nature he was indifferent to those constitutional and fiscal questions upon which the Civil Wars so largely turned; Hampden, Eliot and Pym seemed to him "no-heroes." He failed to understand certain aspects of Puritanism. He was not interested, as his *French Revolution* had already proved, in the systematic, patient exposition of historical fact. Save for the elaborate and matchless picture of the battle of Dunbar, there is scarcely a piece of "set composition"—such as the execution of Charles I or the flight of Charles II might have furnished—in the three volumes. The style has no key-note, unless one is to be discovered in the brief lyrical interludes pathetically apostrophising "my brave Oliver" in the final volume.

What then do we have? Let us listen to W. A. Shaw, one of the recent editors of the work: "With or without his will, and possibly even without his being aware of it—such is the superb art of the book—the reader is reading, not the words of a latter-day historian, not a tale that is told, but the living, spoken word of the protagonist in that mighty conflict. What other book has ever thus revivified the dry bones of historical material? What other book has ever compelled the unwilling millions to listen to the very tones of the voice of a dead hero, to stand face to face to him in the flesh, to know him from the standpoint not of our day but of his own? Answer there is none, for herein the book has no compeer. By the side of the imaginative effect thus wrought, by the side of the naked and imperious truth of such self-portrayal, the ordinary art of the mere historian or of the mere biographer would have been fatuity."

In other words, Carlyle's personal relation to his authorities and hero has such magical vividness that we ourselves see men and objects as if we were physically present. It is "*my* brave Oliver." Mark Noble, one of Carlyle's authorities, is addressed as "my imbecile friend"; Bulstrode, another authority, has a "fat, terrene mind," and we are made to feel it as by physical contact. The books which Carlyle used in writing his *Cromwell*—like the books used in the preparation of his *Frederick*—were presented by him to the Harvard library, and the marginal comments are full of these personal exclamations of admiration or of disgust. And what is true of Carlyle's attitude toward his authorities is still more significantly true of his attitude toward the historic events themselves. He is present, as spectator and listener. " 'I never saw such a charge of boot and horse,' says one; *nor did I.*" Upon Cromwell's dismission of the Rump Parliament "They all vanished; *flooding gloomily clamourously out.*" Now, as Mr. Kipling says: "How does the picture-man know?" That question is of course unanswerable,— but no one ever read Carlyle's *Cromwell* without feeling that this picture-man does know, because he was there!

Of the importance of the contribution thus made to English history, Froude is surely competent to speak:

"This book is, in my opinion, by far the most important contribution to English history which has been made in the present century. Carlyle was the first to break the crust which has overlaid the subject of Cromwell since the Restoration, and to make

Cromwell and Cromwell's age intelligible to mankind. Any one who will read what was written about him before Carlyle's work appeared, and what has been written since, will perceive how great was the achievement. The enthusiast, led away by ambition, and degenerating into the hypocrite, the received figure of the established legend, is gone forever. We may retain each our own opinion about Cromwell, we may think that he did well or that he did ill, that he was wise or unwise; but we see the real man. We can entertain no shadow of doubt about the genuineness of the portrait; and, with the clear sight of Oliver himself, we have a new conception of the Civil War and of its consequences. The book itself carries marks of the difficulty with which it was written. It has no clear continuity; large gaps are left in the story. Contrary to his own rule, that the historian should confine himself to the facts, with the minimum of commentary, Carlyle breaks in repeatedly in his own person, pats his friends upon the back, expands, applauds, criticises to an extent which most readers would wish more limited. This, however, is to be remembered, that he was reproducing letters and speeches, of which both the thought and the lan-

guage were obsolete—obsolete, or worse than obsolete, for most of it had degenerated into cant, in-
sincere in every one who uses such expressions now,
and therefor suggesting insincerity in those who
used them then. Perhaps he allowed too little for
our ability to think for ourselves. But he had seen
how fatally through this particular cause the character of the Commonwealth leaders had been obscured, and, if he erred at all, he erred on the right
side. It is his supreme merit that he first understood
the speeches made by Cromwell in Parliament, and
enabled us to understand them. Printed as they
had hitherto been, they could only confirm the impression, either that the Protector's own mind was
hopelessly confused, or that he purposely concealed
what was in it. Carlyle has shown that they were
perfectly genuine speeches, not eloquent, as modern
parliamentary speeches are, or aspire to be thought;
but the faithful expressions of a most real and determined meaning, about which those who listened to
him could not have been left in doubt at all. Such
a feat was nothing less than extraordinary. It was
not a 'whitewashing,' as attempts of this kind are
often scornfully and sometimes deservedly called.
It was the recovery of a true human figure of im-

mense historical consequence from below two centuries of accumulated slander and misconception,
and the work was completely done. No hammering
or criticising has produced the least effect upon it.
There once more Cromwell stands actually before
us, and henceforth will stand, as he was when he
lived upon the earth. He may be loved or he may
be hated, as he was both loved and hated in his
own time; but we shall love or hate the man himself, not a shadow or a caricature any more."

The Battle of Dunbar

"The small Town of Dunbar stands, high and
windy, looking down over its herring-boats, over
its grim old Castle now much honeycombed,—on one
of those projecting rock-promontories with which
that shore of the Frith of Forth is niched and van-
dyked, as far as the eye can reach. A beautiful sea;
good land too, now that the plougher understands
his trade; a grim niched barrier of whinstone shel-
tering it from the chafings and tumblings of the big
blue German Ocean. Seaward St. Abb's Head, of
whinstone, bounds your horizon to the east, not
very far off; west, close by, is the deep bay, and
fishy little village of Belhaven: the gloomy Bass

and other rock-islets, and farther the Hills of Fife, and foreshadows of the Highlands, are visible as you look seaward. From the bottom of Belhaven Bay to that of the next sea-bight St. Abb's-ward, the Town and its environs form a peninsula. Along the base of which peninsula, 'not much above a mile and a half from sea to sea,' Oliver Cromwell's Army, on Monday 2d of September 1650, stands ranked, with its tents and Town behind it,—in very forlorn circumstances. This now is all the ground that Oliver is lord of in Scotland. His ships lie in the offing, with biscuit and transport for him: but visible elsewhere in the Earth no help.

"Landward as you look from the Town of Dunbar there rises, some short mile off, a dusky continent of barren heath Hills; the Lammermoor, where only mountain-sheep can be at home. The crossing of *which,* by any of its boggy passes, and brawling stream-courses, no Army, hardly a solitary Scotch Packman could attempt, in such weather. To the edge of these Lammermoor Heights, David Lesley has betaken himself; lies now along the outmost spur of them,—a long Hill of considerable height, which the Dunbar people call the Dun, Doon, or sometimes for fashion's sake the Down, adding

to it the Teutonic *Hill* likewise, though *Dun* itself
in old Celtic signifies Hill. On this Doon Hill lies
David Lesley with the victorious Scotch Army, upwards of Twenty-thousand strong; with the Com-
mittees of Kirk and Estates, the chief Dignitaries
of the Country, and in fact the flower of what the
pure Covenant in this the Twelfth year of its existence can still bring forth. There lies he since Sunday night on the top and slope of this Doon Hill,
with the impassable heath-continents behind him;
embraces, as within outspread tiger-claws, the base-
line of Oliver's Dunbar peninsula; waiting what
Oliver will do. Cockburnspath with its ravines
has been seized on Oliver's left, and made impassable; behind Oliver is the sea; in front of him Lesley, Doon Hill, and the heath-continent of Lammermoor. Lesley's force is of Three-and-twenty-
thousand, in spirits as of men chasing, Oliver's
about half as many, in spirits as of men chased.
What is to become of Oliver? . . .

"The base of Oliver's 'Dunbar Peninsula,' as we
have called it (or Dunbar Pinfold where he is now
hemmed in, upon 'an entanglement very difficult'),
extends from Belhaven Bay on his right, to Brocksmouth House on his left; 'about a mile and a half

from sea to sea.' Brocksmouth House, the Earl
(now Duke) of Roxsburgh's mansion, which still
stands there, his soldiers now occupy at their extreme post on the left. As its name indicates, it is
the *mouth* or issue of a small Rivulet, or Burn, called
Brock, Brocksburn; which, springing from the Lammermoor, and skirting David Lesley's Doon Hill,
finds its egress here into the sea. The reader who
would form an image to himself of the great Tuesday 3d of September 1650, at Dunbar, must note
well this little *Burn.* It runs in a deep grassy glen,
which the South-country Officers in those old
Pamphlets describe as a 'deep *ditch,* forty feet in
depth, and about as many in width,'—ditch dug out
by the little Brook itself, and carpeted with greensward, in the course of long thousands of years.
It runs pretty close by the foot of Doon Hill;
forms, from this point to the sea, the boundary of
Oliver's position; his force is arranged in battle-
order along the left bank of this Brocksburn, and
its grassy glen; he is busied all Monday, he and his
Officers, in ranking them there. 'Before sunrise on
Monday' Lesley sent down his horse from the Hill-
top, to occupy the other side of this Brook; 'about
four in the afternoon' his train came down, his

whole Army gradually came down; and they now are ranking themselves on the opposite side of Brocksburn,—on rather narrow ground; cornfields, but swiftly sloping upwards to the steep of Doon Hill. This goes on, in the wild showers and winds of Monday 2d September 1650, on both sides of the Rivulet of Brock. Whoever will begin the attack, must get across this Brook and its glen first; a thing of much disadvantage.

"Behind Oliver's ranks, between him and Dunbar, stand his tents; sprinkled up and down, by battalions, over the face of this 'Peninsula;' which is a low though very uneven tract of ground; now in our time all yellow with wheat and barley in the autumn season, but at that date only partially tilled, —describable by Yorkshire Hodgson as a place of plashes and rough bent-grass; terribly beaten by showery winds that day, so that your tent will hardly stand. There was then but one Farm-house on this tract, where now are not a few: thither were Oliver's Cannon sent this morning; they had at first been lodged 'in the Church,' an edifice standing then as now somewhat apart, 'at the south end of Dunbar.' We have notice of only one other 'small house,' belike some poor shepherd's homestead, in

Oliver's tract of ground: it stands close by the Brock Rivulet itself, and in the bottom of the little glen; at a place where the banks of it flatten themselves out into a slope passable for carts: this of course, as the one 'pass' in that quarter, it is highly important to seize. Pride and Lambert lodged 'six horse and fifteen foot' in this poor hut early in the morning: Lesley's horse came across, and drove them out; killing some and 'taking three prisoners;' —and so got possession of this pass and hut; but did not keep it. Among the three prisoners was one musketeer, 'a very stout man, though he has but a wooden arm,' and some iron hook at the end of it, poor fellow. He 'fired thrice,' not without effect, with his wooden arm; and was not taken without difficulty: a handfast stubborn man; they carried him across to General Lesley to give some account of himself. In several of the old Pamphlets, which agree in all the details of it, this is what we read:

" 'General *David* Lesley (old Leven,' the other Lesley, 'being in the Castle of Edinburgh, as they relate), asked this man, If the Enemy did intend to fight? He replied, 'What do you think we come here for? We come for nothing else!'—'Soldier,' says Lesley, 'how will you fight, when you have

shipped half of your men, and all your great guns?'
The Soldier replied, 'Sir, if you please to draw
your men, you shall find both men and great guns
too!'—A most dogged handfast man, this with the
wooden arm, and iron hook on it! One of the
Officers asked, How he durst answer the General
so saucily? He said, 'I only answer the question
put to me!"' Lesley sent him across, free again, by
a trumpet: he made his way to Cromwell; reported
what had passed, and added doggedly, He for one
had lost twenty shillings by the business,—plundered
from him in this action. 'The Lord General gave
him thereupon two pieces,' which I think are forty
shillings; and sent him away rejoicing.—This is the
adventure at the 'pass' by the shepherd's hut in the
bottom of the glen, close by the Brocksburn itself.

"And now farther, on the great scale, we are to
remark very specially that there is just one other
'pass' across the Brocksburn; and this is precisely
where the London road now crosses it; about a mile
east from the former pass, and perhaps two gun-
shots west from Brocksmouth House. There the
great road then as now crosses the Burn of Brock;
the steep grassy glen, or 'broad ditch forty feet

deep,' flattening itself out here once more into a passable slope: passable, but still steep on the southern or Lesley side, still mounting up there, with considerable acclivity, into a high table-ground, out of which the Doon Hill, as outskirt of the Lammermoor, a short mile to your right, gradually gathers itself. There, at this 'pass,' on and about the present London road, as you discover after long dreary dim examining, took place the brunt or essential agony of the Battle of Dunbar long ago. Read in the extinct old Pamphlets, and ever again obstinately read, till some light rise in them, look even with unmilitary eyes at the ground as it now is, you do at last obtain small glimmerings of distinct features here and there,—which gradually coalesce into a kind of image for you; and some spectrum of the Fact becomes visible; rises veritable, face to face, on you, grim and sad in the depths of the old dead Time. Yes, my travelling friends, vehiculating in gigs or otherwise over that piece of London road, you may say to yourselves, Here without monument is the grave of a valiant thing which was done under the Sun; the footprint of a Hero, not yet quite undistinguishable, is here!—

"'The Lord General about four o'clock,' say the

old Pamphlets, 'went into the Town to take some refreshment,' a hasty late dinner, or early supper, whichever we may call it; 'and very soon returned back,'—having written Sir Arthur's Letter, I think, in the interim. Coursing about the field, with enough of things to order; walking at last with Lambert in the Park or Garden of Brocksmouth House, he discerns that Lesley is astir on the Hillside; altering his position somewhat. That Lesley in fact is coming wholly down to the basis of the Hill, where his horse had been since sunrise: coming wholly down to the edge of the Brook and glen, among the sloping harvest-fields there; and also is bringing up his left wing of horse, most part of it, towards his right; edging himself, 'shogging,' as Oliver calls it, his whole line more and more to the right! His meaning is, to get hold of Brocksmouth House and the pass of the Brook there; after which it will be free to him to attack us when he will!— Lesley, in fact, considers, or at least the Committee of Estates and Kirk consider, that Oliver is lost; that, on the whole, he must not be left to retreat, but must be attacked and annihilated here. A vague story, due to Bishop Burnet, the watery source of many such, still circulates about the world, That it was the Kirk Committee who forced Lesley down against his will; that Oliver, at sight of it, exclaimed, 'The Lord hath delivered' &c.: which nobody is in the least bound to believe. It appears, from other quarters, that Lesley *was* advised or sanctioned in this attempt by the Committee of Estates and Kirk, but also that he was by no means hard to advise; that, in fact, lying on top of Doon Hill, shelterless in such weather, was no operation to spin out beyond necessity;—and that if anybody pressed too much upon him with advice to come down and fight, it was likeliest to be Royalist Civil Dignitaries, who had plagued him with the cavillings at his cunctations, at his 'secret fellow-feeling for the Sectarians and Regicides,' ever since this War began. The poor Scotch Clergy have enough of their own to answer for in this business; let every back bear the burden that belongs to it. In a word, Lesley descends, has been descending all day, and 'shogs' himself to the right,—urged, I believe, by manifold counsel, and by the nature of the case; and, what is equally important for us, Oliver sees him, and sees through him, in this movement of his.

"At sight of this movement, Oliver suggests to Lambert standing by him, Does it not give *us* an advantage, if we, instead of him, like to begin the attack? Here is the Enemy's right wing coming out to the open space, free to be attacked on any side; and the main-battle, hampered in narrow sloping ground between Doon Hill and the Brook, has no room to manœuvre or assist: beat this right wing where it now stands; take it in flank and front with an overpowering force,—it is driven upon its own main-battle, the whole army is beaten? Lambert eagerly assents, 'had meant to say the same thing.' Monk, who comes up at the moment, likewise assents; as the other Officers do, when the case is set before them. It is the plan resolved upon for battle. The attack shall begin tomorrow before dawn.

"And so the soldiers stand to their arms, or lie within instant reach of their arms, all night; being upon an engagement very difficult indeed. The night is wild and wet;—2d of September means 12th by our calender: the Harvest Moon wades deep among clouds of sleet and hail. Whoever has a heart for prayer, let him pray now, for the wrestle of death is at hand. Pray,—and withal keep his powder dry! And be ready for extremities, and quit himself like a man!—Thus they pass the night; making that Dunbar Peninsula and Brook Rivulet long memorable to me. We English have some tents; the Scots have none. The hoarse sea moans bodeful, swinging low and heavy against these whinstone bays; the sea and the tempests are abroad, all else asleep but we,—and there is One that rides on the wings of the wind.

"Towards three in the morning the Scotch foot, by order of a Major-General say some, extinguish their matches, all but two in a company; cower under the corn-shocks, seeking some imperfect shelter and sleep. Be wakeful, ye English; watch, and pray, and keep your powder dry. About four o'clock comes order to my puddingheaded Yorkshire friend, that his regiment must mount and march straightway; his and various other regiments march, pouring swiftly to the left to Brocksmouth House, to the Pass over the Brock. With overpowering force let us storm the Scots right wing there; beat that, and all is beaten. Major Hodgson riding along, heard, he says, 'a Cornet praying in the night;' a company of poor men, I think, making worship there, under the void Heaven, before battle joined: Major Hodgson, giving his charge to a brother Officer, turned aside to listen for a minute, and worship and pray along with them; haply his

last prayer on this Earth, as it might prove to be.
But no: this Cornet prayed with such effusion as
was wonderful; and imparted strength to my Yorkshire friend, who strengthened his men by telling
them of it.   And the Heavens, in their mercy, I
think, have opened us a way of deliverance!—The
Moon gleams out, hard and blue, riding among hail-
clouds; and over St. Abb's Head a streak of dawn is
rising.

"And now is the hour when the attack should be,
and no Lambert is yet here, he is ordering the line
far to the right yet; and Oliver occasionally, in
Hodgson's hearing, is impatient for him.   The Scots
too, on this wing, are awake; thinking to surprise
us; there is their trumpet sounding, we heard it
once; and Lambert, who was to lead the attack, is
not here.   The Lord General is impatient;—behold
Lambert at last!   The trumpets peal, shattering with
fierce clangour Night's silence; the cannons awaken
along all the Line: 'The Lord of Hosts! The Lord
of Hosts!'   On, my brave ones, on!—

"The dispute 'on this right wing was hot and
stiff, for three quarters of an hour.'   Plenty of fire,
from fieldpieces, snaphances, matchlocks, enter-
tains the Scotch main-battle across the Brock;—

poor stiffened men, roused from the corn-shocks
with their matches all out! But here on the right,
their horse, 'with lancers in the front rank,' charge
desperately; drive us back across the hollow of the
Rivulet;—back a little; but the Lord gives us
courage, and we storm home again, horse and foot,
upon them, with a shock like tornado tempests;
break them, beat them, drive them all adrift. 'Some
fled towards Copperspath, but most across their
own foot.' Their own poor foot, whose matches
were hardly well alight yet! Poor men, it was a
terrible awakening for them: fieldpieces and charge
of foot across the Brocksburn; and now here is
their own horse in mad panic trampling them to
death. Above Three-thousand killed upon the place:
'I never saw such a charge of foot and horse,' says
one; nor did I. Oliver was still near to Yorkshire
Hodgson when the shock succeeded; Hodgson heard
him say, 'They run! I profess they run!' And over
St. Abb's Head and the German Ocean, just then,
bursts the first gleam of the level Sun upon us,
'and I heard Nol say, in the words of the Psalmist,
"Let God arise, let His enemies be scattered," '—or
in Rous's metre,

> "Let God arise, and scattered
> Let all his enemies be;
> And let all those that do him hate
> Before his presence flee!"

"Even so. The Scotch Army is shivered to utter ruin; rushes in tumultuous wreck, hither, thither; to Belhaven, or, in their distraction, even to Dunbar, the chase goes as far as Haddington; led by Hacker. 'The Lord General made a halt,' says Hodgson, 'and sang the Hundred-and-seventeenth Psalm,' till our horse could gather for the chase. Hundred-and-seventeenth Psalm at the foot of the Doon Hill; there we uplift it, to the tune of Bangor, or some still higher score, and roll it strong and great against the sky:

> "O give ye praise unto the Lord,
> All nati-ons that be;
> Likewise ye people all, accord
> His name to magnify!

> "For great to-us-ward ever are
> His lovingkindnesses;
> His truth endures forevermore;
> The Lord O do ye bless!"

And now, to the chase again.

"The Prisoners are Ten-thousand,—all the foot

in a mass. Many Dignitaries are taken; not a few
are slain; of whom see Printed Lists,—full of blun-
ders. Provost Jaffray of Aberdeen, Member of the
Scots Parliament, one of the Committee of Estates,
was very nearly slain; a trooper's sword was in the
air to sever him, but one cried, He is a man of consequence; he can ransom himself!—and the trooper
kept him prisoner. The first of the Scots Quakers,
by and by; and an official person much reconciled to
Oliver. Ministers also of the Kirk Committee were
slain; two Ministers I find taken, poor Carstairs of
Glasgow, poor Waugh of some other place,—of
whom we shall transiently hear again.

"General David Lesley, vigourous for flight as for
other things, got to Edinburgh by nine o'clock; poor
old Leven, not so light of movement, did not get
there till two. Tragical enough. What a change
since January 1644, when we marched out of this
same Dunbar up to the knees in snow! It was to
help and save these very men that we then marched;
with the Covenant in all our hearts. We have stood
by the letter of the Covenant; fought for our Cov-
enanted Stuart King as we could;—they again, they
stand by the substance of it, and have trampled us
and the letter of it into this ruinous state!—Yes, my

poor friends;—and now be wise, be taught! The letter of your Covenant, in fact, will never rally again in this world. The spirit and substance of it, please God, will never die in this or in any world.

"Such is Dunbar Battle; which might also be called Dunbar Drove, for it was a frightful rout. Brought on by miscalculation; misunderstanding of the difference between substances and semblances; —by mismanagement, and the chance of war."

CHAPTER XVI

LATTER-DAY PAMPHLETS

CARLYLE'S final opinion of contemporary politics dates from 1850; the year when Jeffrey and Wordsworth and Peel died, and Tennyson published *In Memoriam,*—the year also of our American "Compromise of 1850," typified in the Fugitive Slave Bill. Up to this time Carlyle had unquestionably cherished some notion of taking part in politics himself. He told Froude that he had thought of entering Parliament "at the time of the *Latter-Day Pamphlets,*" and he still hoped much from the leadership of Sir Robert Peel, whose death by accident in June, 1850, while the *Pamphlets* were still publishing, seemed to Carlyle to be the final adverse stroke of fate. But his real motive in issuing the *Pamphlets* was not so much to affect public opinion as, in his own words, "to give vent to myself." He forgot, as he did habitually, his wise admonition to Emerson, "A man has no

223

right to say to his own generation, turning quite
away from it, 'Be damned!'" And saying it now
to his heart's relief, he was little surprised at the
natural result upon his audience.

"You never in your life," he wrote to his farmer
brother Alexander, "heard such a screaming and
squealing,—a universal 'screigh (screech) as of
stuck pigs.'" But his deliverances caused not
merely anger, but what was even more fatal to his
reputation for political wisdom, namely, amuse-
ment. Laughter is perhaps the deadliest retort of
the political debater, and most Englishmen con-
tented themselves by laughing at Carlyle's extrava-
gances. Mill, who had little sense of humor, took
Carlyle seriously enough. When the prelude to the
Pamphlets, the "Occasional Discourse on the Nigger
Question," was printed in *Fraser's* in December,
1849, Mill, shocked by Carlyle's defense of negro
slavery and praise of the beneficent whip, replied in
Fraser's for January, 1850, to the effect that Carlyle's doctrine of "born servants" was a "damnable
doctrine," and that it was "a true work of the devil
to throw this missile into the Abolition camp in
America." This article was signed "D"; Carlyle
thought it "most shrill, thin, poor and insignificant,"

but read to-day, it is obvious that Mill's position was not only significant, but right.

In February Carlyle printed, not in *Fraser's* but independently, the first of his eight *Pamphlets,* on *The Present Time.* It contained the famous metaphor of the ship doubling Cape Horn by ballot.

"Your ship can not double Cape Horn by its excellent plans of voting. The ship may vote this and that, above decks and below, in the most harmonious exquisitely constitutional manner: the ship, to get round Cape Horn, will find a set of conditions already voted for, and fixed with adamantine rigour by the ancient Elemental Powers, who are entirely careless how you vote. It you can, by voting or without voting, ascertain these conditions, and valiantly conform to them, you will get round the Cape: if you can not,—the ruffian Winds will blow you ever back again; the inexorable Icebergs, dumb privy-councillors from Chaos, will nudge you with most chaotic 'admonition'; you will be flung half frozen on the Patagonian cliffs, or admonished into shivers by your iceberg councillors, and sent sheer down to Davy Jones, and will never get round Cape Horn at all! Unanimity on board ship;—yes indeed, the ship's crew may be very unanimous, which doubtless, for the time being, will be very comfortable to the ship's crew, and to their Phantasm Captain if they have one: but if the tack they unanimously steer upon is guiding them into the belly of the Abyss, it will not profit them much!— Ships accordingly do not use the ballot-box at all; and they reject the Phantasm species of Captains: one wishes much some other Entities—since all entities lie under the same rigourous set of laws—could be brought to show as much wisdom, and sense at least of self-preservation, the first command of Nature. Phantasm Captains with unanimous votings: this is considered to be all the law and all the prophets, at present."

The few Wise, in short, will have to take command of the innumerable Foolish; that is the essence of the first *Pamphlet*. The second, based upon a recent visit to a Model Prison, breathes a "healthy hatred of scoundrels," a Hebraic "irreconcilable inexorable enmity to the enemies of God." This is excellent Carlylese matter, provided one is sure that he is on the Lord's side! The third *Pamphlet* is on *Downing Street,* and again there is a splendid naval metaphor, in the symbolical style of Burke:

"Can anything be more unreasonable than a Seventy-four? Articulately almost nothing. But it has inarticulate traditions, ancient methods and habitudes in it, stoicisms, noblenesses, true rules both of sailing and of conduct; enough to keep it afloat on Nature's veridical bosom, after all. See; if you bid it to sail to the end of the world, it will lift anchor, go, and arrive. The raging oceans do not beat it back; it too, as well as the raging oceans, has a relationship to Nature, and it does not sink, but under the due conditions is borne along. If it meet with hurricanes, it rides them out; if it meet an Enemy's ship, it shivers it to powder; and in short, it holds on its way, and to a wonderful extent does what it means and pretends to do. Assure yourself, my friend, there is an immense fund of truth somewhere or other stowed in that Seventy-four."

But instead of this superb emblem of national progress, England has, alas, a Phantasm at the helm: "an eyeless Pilot with constitutional spectacles, steering by the ear," or, as we say in our American vernacular, a politician with his ear to the ground. Peel indeed,—whom Carlyle had just met,—had accomplished, in his repeal of the Corn

Laws, "the largest veracity ever *done* in Parliament in our time." These words were published in April, and in two months Peel was dead. In the interval Carlyle went on, attacking Oratory and Parliaments, and celebrating once more his "undistributed middle"—the cause of most of his fallacies —namely that Nature of Things which unluckily is usually only what you and I conceive the Nature of Things to be, and may not be in reality the Nature of Things at all!

As the *Pamphlets* draw to a close, Carlyle's bitterness increases. "We are a lost gregarious horde, presided over by the Anarch Old." "All art and industry is tainted." With the power of a Swift he paints the Universe as an immeasurable Swine's trough, and composes a catechism of the Whole Duty of Pigs. And yet he does not end upon this note, but rather in the old and for Carlyle the fundamental *Sartor* key,—namely that "God did make this world, and does forever govern it;" that "Time does rest on Eternity; that he who has no vision of Eternity will never get a true hold of Time, or its affairs." His final injunction then is to Do Nobly, ere the night cometh wherein no man can work. Otherwise humanity will remain under a curse.

"Mount into your railways; whirl from place to place, at the rate of fifty, or if you like of five hundred miles an hour: you can not escape from that inexorable all-encircling ocean-moan of ennui. No: if you would mount to the stars, and do yacht-voyages under the belts of Jupiter, or stalk deer on the ring of Saturn, it would still begirdle you. You can not escape from it, you can but change your place in it, without solacement except one moment's. That prophetic Sermon from the deeps will continue with you, till you wisely interpret it and do it, or else till the Crack of Doom swallow it and you. *Adieu: Au revoir.*"

CHAPTER XVII

THE LIFE OF JOHN STERLING

NOT to know Carlyle's *Life of John Sterling* is to overlook one of the most perfect examples of his literary art. Those readers particularly who regard Carlyle as primarily a prophet and teacher ought, from time to time, to turn again the pages of this charming biography, in order to renew their impressions of Carlyle's mastery of word and phrase, his sensitiveness to landscape, his knack of portrait-painting, and above all his sincerity and tenderness of friendship.

Sterling, who died in 1844 after a brief career in the Church and as a man of letters, was a singularly attractive person. Archdeacon Hare, who with Carlyle had acted as Sterling's literary executor, had produced a biography which seemed to Carlyle too full of ecclesiastical matters to do full justice to Sterling's many-sided sympathies. Accordingly he set himself, in 1851, to some "swift scrib-

230

bling" in order to redress the balance. "Here, visible to myself, for some while, was a brilliant human presence, distinguishable, honourable and lovable amid the dim common populations; among the million little beautiful, once more a beautiful human soul: whom I, among others, recognized and lovingly walked with, while the years and the hours were. Sitting now by his tomb in thoughtful mood, the new times bring a new duty to me. 'Why write the Life of Sterling?' I imagine I had a commission higher than the world's, the dictate of Nature herself, to do what is now done. *Sic prosit.*"

The grace and perfection of Carlyle's performance can not adequately be indicated by random quotations, but we must at least make room for the inimitable picture of Coleridge at Highgate, familiar though it be to many persons who have never given themselves the pleasure of reading *The Life of Sterling* as a whole.

Coleridge

"Coleridge sat on the brow of Highgate Hill, in those years, looking down on London and its smoke-tumult, like a sage escaped from the inanity of life's battle; attracting towards him the thoughts of innumerable brave souls still engaged there. His express contributions to poetry, philosophy, or any specific province of human literature or enlightenment, had been small and sadly intermittent; but he had, especially among young inquiring men, a higher than literary, a kind of prophetic or magician character. He was thought to hold, he alone in England, the key of German and other Transcendentalisms; knew the sublime secret of believing by 'the reason' what 'the understanding' had been obliged to fling out as incredible; and could still, after Hume and Voltaire had done their best and worst with him, profess himself an orthodox Christian, and say and print to the Church of England, with its singular old rubrics and surplices at Allhallowtide, *Esto perpetua.* A sublime man; who, alone in those dark days, had saved his crown of spiritual manhood; escaping from the black materialisms, and revolutionary deluges, with 'God, Freedom, Immortality' still his: a king of men. The practical intellects of the world did not much heed him, or carelessly reckoned him a metaphysical dreamer: but to the rising spirits of the young generation he had this dusky sublime character; and sat there as a kind of *Magus,* girt in mystery and enigma; his

Dodona oak-grove (Mr. Gilman's house at Highgate) whispering strange things, uncertain whether
oracles or jargon.

"The Gilmans did not encourage much company,
or excitation of any sort, round their sage; nevertheless access to him, if a youth did reverently wish
it, was not difficult. He would stroll about the
pleasant garden with you, sit in the pleasant rooms
of the place,—perhaps take you to his own peculiar
room, high up, with a rearward view, which was
the chief view of all. A really charming outlook,
in fine weather. Close at hand, wide sweep of
flowery leafy gardens, their few houses mostly hidden, the very chimney-pots veiled under blossomy
umbrage, flowed gloriously down hill; gloriously
issuing in wide-tufted undulating plain-country, rich
in all charms of field and town. Waving blooming
country of the brightest green; dotted all over with
handsome villas, handsome groves; crossed by roads
and human traffic, here inaudible or heard only as
a musical hum: and behind all swam, under olive-
tinted haze, the illimitable limitary ocean of London, with its domes and steeples definite in the sun,
big Paul's and the many memories attached to it
hanging high over all. Nowhere, of its kind, could

you see a grander prospect on a bright summer day, with the set of the air going southward,—southward, and so draping with the city-smoke not *you* but the city. Here for hours would Coleridge talk, concerning all conceivable or inconceivable things; and liked nothing better than to have an intelligent, or failing that, even a silent and patient human listener. He distinguished himself to all that ever heard him as at least the most surprising talker extant in this world,—and to some small minority, by no means to all, as the most excellent.

"The good man, he was now getting old, towards sixty perhaps; and gave you the idea of a life that had been full of sufferings; a life heavy-laden, half-vanquished, still swimming painfully in seas of manifold physical and other bewilderment. Brow and head were round, and of massive weight, but the face was flabby and irresolute. The deep eyes, of a light hazel, were as full of sorrow as of inspiration; confused pain looked timidly from them, as in a kind of mild astonishment. The whole figure and air, good and amiable otherwise, might be called flabby and irresolute; expressive of weakness under possibility of strength. He hung loosely on his limbs, with knees bent, and stooping attitude; in walking, he rather shuffled than decisively stept; and a lady once remarked, he never could fix which side of the garden-walk would suit him best, but continually shifted, in corkscrew fashion, and kept trying both. A heavy-laden, high-aspiring and surely much-suffering man. His voice, naturally soft and good, had contracted itself into a plaintive snuffle and singsong; he spoke as if preaching,—you would have said, preaching earnestly and also hopelessly the weightiest things. I still recollect his 'object' and 'subject,' terms of continual recurrence in the Kantean province; and how he sung and snuffled them into 'om-m-mject' and 'sum-m-mject,' with a kind of solemn shake or quaver, as he rolled along. No talk, in his century or in any other, could be more surprising.

"Sterling, who assiduously attended him, with profound reverence, and was often with him by himself, for a good many months, gives a record of their first colloquy.[1] Their colloquies were numerous, and he had taken note of many; but they are all gone to the fire, except this first, which Mr. Hare has printed,—unluckily without date. It contains a number of ingenious, true and halftrue ob-

---

[1] Biography by Hare, pp. xvi -xxvi.

servations, and is of course a faithful epitome of the things said; but it gives small idea of Coleridge's way of talking;—this one feature is perhaps the most recognisable, 'Our interview lasted for three hours, during which he talked two hours and three quarters.' Nothing could be more copious than his talk; and furthermore it was always, virtually or literally, of the nature of a monologue; suffering no interruption, however reverent; hastily putting aside all foreign additions, annotations, or most ingenuous desires for elucidation, as well-meant superfluities which would never do. Besides, it was a talk not flowing anywhither like a river, but spreading everywhither in inextricable currents and regurgitations like a lake or sea; terribly deficient in definite goal or aim, nay often in logical intelligibility; *what* you were to believe or do, on any earthly or heavenly thing, obstinately refusing to appear from it. So that, most times, you felt logically lost; swamped near to drowning in this tide of ingenious vocables, spreading out boundless as if to submerge the world.

"To sit as a passive bucket and be pumped into, whether you consent or not, can in the long-run be exhilarating to no creature; how eloquent soever

the flood of utterance that is descending. But if it
be withal a confused unintelligible flood of utterance, threatening to submerge all known landmarks
of thought, and drown the world and you!—I have
heard Coleridge talk, with eager musical energy, two
stricken hours, his face radiant and moist, and communicate no meaning whatsoever to any individual
of his hearers,—certain of whom, I for one, still
kept eagerly listening in hope; the most had long
before given up, and formed (if the room were large
enough) secondary humming groups of their own.
He began anywhere: you put some question to him,
made some suggestive observation: instead of an-
swering this, or decidedly setting out towards answer of it, he would accumulate formidable appa-
ratus, logical swim-bladders, transcendental life-
preservers and other precautionary and vehicula-
tory gear, for setting out; perhaps did at last get
under way,—but was swiftly solicited, turned aside
by the glance of some radiant new game on this
hand or that, into new courses; and ever into new;
and before long into all the Universe, where it was
uncertain what game you would catch, or whether
any.

"His talk, alas, was distinguished, like himself,

by irresolution: it disliked to be troubled with conditions, abstinences, definite fulfilments;—loved to
wander at its own sweet will, and make its auditor
and his claims and humble wishes a mere passive
bucket for itself! He had knowledge about many
things and topics, much curious reading; but generally all topics led him, after a pass or two, into
the high seas of theosophic philosophy, the hazy
infinitude of Kantean transcendentalism, with its
'sum-m-jects' and 'om-m-mjects.' Sad enough; for
with such indolent impatience of the claims and
ignorances of others, he had not the least talent for
explaining this or anything unknown to them; and
you swam and fluttered in the mistiest wide unintelligible deluge of things, for most part in a rather
profitless uncomfortable manner.

"Glorious islets, too, I have seen rise out of the
haze; but they were few, and soon swallowed in
the general element again. Balmy sunny islets,
islets of the blest and the intelligible:—on which
occasions those secondary humming groups would
all cease humming, and hang breathless upon the
eloquent words; till once your islet got wrapt in the
mist again, and they could recommence humming.
Eloquent artistically expressive words you always

had; piercing radiances of a most subtle insight came at intervals; tones of noble pious sympathy, recognisable as pious though strangely coloured, were never wanting long: but in general you could not call this aimless, cloudcapt, cloudbased, lawlessly meandering human discourse of reason by the name of 'excellent talk,' but only of 'surprising;' and were reminded bitterly of Hazlitt's account of it: 'Excellent talker, very,—if you let him start from no premises and come to no conclusion.' Coleridge was not without what talkers call wit, and there were touches of prickly sarcasm in him, contemptuous enough of the world and its idols and popular dignitaries; he had traits even of poetic humour: but in general he seemed deficient in laughter; or indeed in sympathy for concrete human things on the sunny or on the stormy side. One right peal of concrete laughter at some convicted flesh-and-blood absurdity, one burst of noble indignation at some injustice or depravity, rubbing elbows with us on this solid Earth, how strange would it have been in that Kantean haze-world, and how infinitely cheering amid its vacant air-castles and dim-melting ghosts and shadows! None such ever came. His life had been an abstract thinking

and dreaming, idealistic, passed amid the ghosts of
defunct bodies and of unborn ones. The moaning
singsong of that theosophico-metaphysical monotony
left on you, at last, a very dreary feeling.

"In close colloquy, flowing within narrower
banks, I suppose he was more definite and appre-
hensible; Sterling in aftertimes did not complain of
his unintelligibility, or imputed it only to the ab-
struse high nature of the topics handled. Let us
hope so, let us try to believe so! There is no doubt
but Coleridge could speak plain words on things
,plain: his observations and responses on the trivial
matters that occurred were as simple as the commonest man's, or were even distinguished by superior simplicity as well as pertinency. 'Ah, your
tea is too cold, Mr. Coleridge!' mourned the good
Mrs. Gilman once, in her kind, reverential and yet
protective manner, handing him a very tolerable
though belated cup.—'It's better than I deserve!'
snuffled he, in a low hoarse murmur, partly cour-
teous, chiefly pious, the tone of which still abides
with me: 'It's better than I deserve!' "

CHAPTER XVIII

FREDERICK THE GREAT

THE disillusioned spirit in which Carlyle planned and executed the last and most formidable of his literary undertakings, has been indicated in an earlier chapter. He had little enthusiasm for his hero, and Luther, whose biography he had thought of writing, would doubtless have proved a more congenial subject. But he perceived, even in the "vulpine" Frederick, something of that blazing insight into the Nature of Things which Carlyle believed to be the divinest of our human faculties. The book, then, is Carlyle's final celebration of what he loved to call the Divine Fact, however darkened and obscured that Fact might be by the confused welter of eighteenth century Europe.

To trace satisfactorily the origins of the Prussian monarchy it was necessary to go far back into the Middle Ages, and to show the full range and significance of Frederick's activities it was essential

that his biographer should keep in view not merely
the evolution of Central Europe in Frederick's day,
but those world-wide happenings which influenced
and illustrated, at this point and that, the details of
Prussian history. Hence the extraordinary scope
of Carlyle's narrative. As Garnett puts it, "Frederick moves in the midst of a multitudinous pageant.
Carlyle has ransacked the earth to fill his train.
'Quae regio terrae nostri non plena laboris?' Mo-
hawks and Moguls swell the host, philosophers jos-
tle opera dancers; nay, the procession is headed by
a troop of Electoral-Spectres, alive for the occasion.
It would be a prodigious historical masquerade were
the characters in domino. But every figure has its
own proper visage, stamped indelibly with the expression it bore as he flitted across this earth.
Everything aids the picture; some things encumber
the history."

The twenty-one Books that contain this vast pic-
ture-history represent thirteen years of Carlyle's
working life, and in bulk they make up about one
third of all his published writing. A "tremendous
book" indeed, as Mrs. Carlyle said! He had the
assistance of two faithful secretaries, and made two
visits to Europe in order to visit in person every

one of Frederick's battle-fields. So vividly accurate were Carlyle's descriptions of his hero's campaigns and battles that for many years after the publication of the work it was used as a text-book by German officers. The triumph of Prussia over France in the war of 1870 contributed greatly to the influence of Carlyle's history, for all Europe wished to learn something from him as to the first forging of that grim military machine which had just crushed France, and which, in the succeeding half-century, has become such a portentous phenomenon to our civilization.

Not many readers of the present volume, it may be supposed, have the leisure requisite for acquainting themselves with Carlyle's *Frederick* in its entirety. But they should at least glance at the titles of the various Books, and admire the provocative, arresting art of the chapter headings. They should read, if possible, the first three books, then the eighteenth,—picturing the climax of the Seven Years War,—and the twenty-first, in which the story is drawn somewhat hurriedly and wearily to a close. The scope of this volume does not admit the presentation of any of the battle scenes. We must likewise omit examples of those "flash-light"

episodes and portraits that give such startling
vividness to these thousands of pages. We must
print merely the picture of Frederick in the opening
chapter, and then turn to the closing scene, where
Carlyle has heard and we may still hear the curtain
rustling down.

Frederick

"About fourscore years ago, there used to be
seen sauntering on the terraces of Sans Souci, for
a short time in the afternoon, or you might have
met him elsewhere at an earlier hour, riding or driving in a rapid business manner on the open roads or
through the scraggy woods and avenues of that intricate amphibious Potsdam region, a highly interesting lean little old man, of alert though slightly
stooping figure; whose name among strangers was
King *Friedrich the Second,* or Frederick the Great
of Prussia, and at home among the common people,
who much loved and esteemed him, was *Vater Fritz,*
—Father Fred,—a name of familiarity which had
not bred contempt in that instance. He is a King
every inch of him, though without the trappings of
a King. Presents himself in a Spartan simplicity
of vesture : no crown but an old military cocked-hat,

—generally old, or trampled and kneaded into absolute *softness,* if new;—no sceptre but one like Agamemnon's, a walking-stick cut from the woods, which serves also as a riding-stick (with which he hits the horse 'between the ears,' say authors);—and for royal robes, a mere soldier's blue coat with red facings, coat likely to be old, and sure to have a good deal of Spanish snuff on the breast of it; rest of the apparel dim, unobtrusive in colour or cut, ending in high over-knee military boots, which may be brushed (and, I hope, kept soft with an underhand suspicion of oil), but are not permitted to be blackened or varnished; Day and Martin with their soot-pots forbidden to approach.

"The man is not of godlike physiognomy, any more than of imposing stature or costume: close-shut mouth with thin lips, prominent jaws and nose, receding brow, by no means of Olympian height; head, however, is of long form, and has superlative gray eyes in it. Not what is called a beautiful man, nor yet, by all appearance, what is called a happy. On the contrary, the face bears evidence of many sorrows, as they are termed, of much hard labour done in this world; and seems to anticipate nothing but more still coming. Quiet stoicism, capable

enough of what joy there were, but not expecting
any worth mention; great unconscious and some
conscious pride, well tempered with a cheery mock-
ery of humour,—are written on that old face; which
carries its chin well forward, in spite of the slight
stoop about the neck; snuffy nose rather flung into
the air, under its old cocked-hat,—like an old snuffy
lion on the watch; and such a pair of eyes no man
or lion or lynx of that Century bore elsewhere, according to all testimony we have. 'Those eyes,'
says Mirabeau, 'which, at the bidding of his great
soul, fascinated you with seduction or with terror
(*portaient au gré de son âme héroïque, la séduction
ou la terreur*).' Most excellent potent brilliant eyes,
swift-darting as the stars, steadfast as the sun; gray,
we said, of the azure-gray colour; large enough,
not of glaring size; the habitual expression of them
vigilance and penetrating sense, rapidity resting on
depth. Which is an excellent combination; and
gives us the notion of a lambent outer radiance
springing from some great inner sea of light and
fire in the man. The voice, if he speak to you, is
of similar physiognomy, clear, melodious and sonorous; all tones are in it, from that of ingenuous
inquiry, graceful sociality, light-flowing banter,

(rather prickly for most part), up to definite word
of command, up to desolating word of rebuke and
reprobation; a voice 'the clearest and most agreeable
in conversation I ever heard,' says witty Dr. Moore.
'He speaks a great deal,' continues the Doctor; 'yet
those who hear him, regret that he does not speak
a good deal more. His observations are always
lively, very often just; and few men possess the
talent of repartee in greater perfection.'

"Just about threescore and ten years ago, his
speakings and his workings came to finis in this
World of Time; and he vanished from all eyes into
other worlds, leaving much inquiry about him in the
minds of men;—which, as my readers and I may
feel too well, is yet by no means satisfied. As to his
speech, indeed, though it had the worth just ascribed
to it and more, and though masses of it were delib-
erately put on paper by himself, in prose and verse,
and continue to be printed and kept legible, what he
spoke has pretty much vanished into the inane; and
except as record or document of what he did, hardly
now concerns mankind. But the things he did were
extremely remarkable; and can not be forgotten by
mankind. Indeed they bear such fruit to the present
hour as all the Newspapers are obliged to be taking

note of, sometimes to an unpleasant degree. Editors vaguely account this man the 'Creator of the Prussian Monarchy;' which has since grown so large in the world, and troublesome to the Editorial mind in this and other countries. He was indeed the first who, in a highly public manner, notified its creation; announced to all men that it was, in very deed, created; standing on its feet there, and would go a great way, on the impulse it had got from him and others. As it has accordingly done; and may still keep doing to lengths little dreamt of by the British Editor in our time; whose prophesyings upon Prussia, and insights into Prussia, in its past, or present or future, are truly as yet inconsiderable, in proportion to the noise he makes with them! The more is the pity for him,—and for myself too in the Enterprise now on hand. . . .

"This was a man of infinite mark to his contemporaries; who had witnessed surprising feats from him in the world; very questionable notions and ways, which he had contrived to maintain against the world and its criticisms. As an original man has always to do; much more an original ruler of men. The world, in fact, had tried hard to put him down, as it does, unconsciously or con-

sciously, with all such; and after the most conscious
exertions, and at one time a dead-lift spasm of all
its energies for Seven Years, had not been able.
Principalities and powers, Imperial, Royal, Czarish,
Papal, enemies innumerable as the sea-sand, had
risen against him, only one helper left among the
world's Potentates (and that one only while there
should be help rendered in return); and he led them
all such a dance as had astonished mankind and
them.

"No wonder they thought him worthy of notice.
Every original man of any magnitude is;—nay, in
the long run, who or what else is? But how much
more if your original man was a king over men;
whose movements were polar, and carried from day
to day those of the world along with them. The
Samson Agonistes,—were his life passed like that
of Samuel Johnson in dirty garrets, and the produce
of it only some bits of written paper,—the
Agonistes, and how he will comport himself in the
Philistine mill; this is always a spectacle of truly
epic and tragic nature. The rather, if your Samson,
royal or other, is not yet blinded or subdued to the
wheel; much more if he vanquish his enemies, *not*
by suicidal methods, but march out at last flourish-

ing his miraculous fighting implement, and leaving their mill and them in quite ruinous circumstances. As this King Friedrich fairly managed to do.

"For he left the world all bankrupt, we may say; fallen into bottomless abysses of destruction; he still in a paying condition, and with footing capable to carry his affairs and him. When he died, in 1786, the enormous Phenomenon since called FRENCH REVOLUTION was already growling audibly in the depths of the world; meteoric-electric coruscations heralding it, all round the horizon. Strange enough to note, one of Friedrich's last visitors was Gabriel Honoré Riquetti, Comte de Mirabeau. These two saw one another; twice, for half-an-hour each time. The last of the old Gods and the first of the modern Titans;—before Pelion leapt on Ossa; and the foul Earth taking fire at last, its vile mephitic elements went up in volcanic thunder. This also is one of the peculiarities of Friedrich, that he is hitherto the last of the Kings; that he ushers in the French Revolution, and closes an Epoch of World-History. Finishing off forever the trade of King, think many; who have grown profoundly dark as to Kingship and him. . . .

"Friedrich is by no means one of the perfect

demi-gods; and there are various things to be said against him with good ground. To the last, a questionable hero; with much in him which one could have wished not there, and much wanting which one could have wished. But there is one feature which strikes you at an early period of the inquiry, That in his way he is a Reality; that he always means what he speaks; grounds his actions, too, on what he recognises for the truth; and, in short, has nothing whatever of the Hypocrite or Phantasm. Which some readers will admit to be an extremely rare phenomenon.

"We perceive that this man was far indeed from trying to deal swindler-like with the facts around him; that he honestly recognised said facts whereever they disclosed themselves, and was very anxious also to ascertain their existence where still hidden or dubious. For he knew well, to a quite uncommon degree, and with a merit all the higher as it was an unconscious one, how entirely inexorable is the nature of facts, whether recognised or not, ascertained or not; how vain all cunning or diplomacy, management and sophistry, to save any mortal who does *not* stand on the truth of things, from sinking, in the longrun. Sinking to the very Mud-

gods, with all his diplomacies, possessions, achieve-
ments; and becoming an unnameable object, hidden
deep in the Cesspools of the Universe. This I hope
to make manifest; this which I long ago discerned
for myself, with pleasure, in the physiognomy of
Friedrich and his life. Which indeed was the first
real sanction, and has all along been my inducement
and encouragement, to study his life and him. How
this man, officially a King withal, comported himself in the Eighteenth Century, and managed *not*
to be a Liar and Charlatan as his Century was, deserves to be seen a little by men and kings, and may
silently have didactic meanings in it."

Frederick's Death

"He well knew himself to be dying; but some
think, expected that the end might be a little farther
off. There is a grand simplicity of stoicism in him;
coming as if by nature, or by long *second*-nature;
finely unconsious of itself, and finding nothing of
peculiar in this new trial lain on it. From of old,
Life has been infinitely contemptible to him. In
death, I think, he has neither fear nor hope.
Atheism, truly, he never could abide: to him, as to
all of us, it was flatly inconceivable that intellect,

moral emotion, could have been put into *him* by an Entity that had none of its own. But there, pretty much, his Theism seems to have stopped. Instinctively, too, he believed, no man more firmly, that Right alone has ultimately any strength in this world: ultimately, yes;—but for him and his poor brief interests, what good was it? Hope for himself in Divine Justice, in Divine Providence, I think he had not practically any; that the unfathomable Demiurgus should concern himself with such a set of paltry ill-given animalcules as oneself and mankind are, this also, as we have often noticed, is in the main incredible to him.

"A sad Creed, this of the King's;—he had to do his duty without fee or reward. Yes, reader;— and what is well worth your attention, you will have difficulty to find, in the annals of any Creed, a King or man who stood more faithfully to his duty; and, till the last hour, alone concerned himself with doing that. To poor Friedrich that was all the Law and all the Prophets: and I much recommend you to surpass him, if you, by good luck, have a better Copy of those inestimable Documents!—Inarticulate notions, fancies, transient aspirations, he might have, in the background of his mind. One day, sitting for a while out of doors, gazing into the Sun, he was heard to murmur, 'Perhaps I shall be nearer thee soon:'—and indeed nobody knows what his thoughts were in these final months. There is traceable only a complete superiority to Fear and Hope; in parts, too, are half-glimpses of a great motionless interior lake of Sorrow, sadder than any tears or complainings, which are altogether wanting to it. . . .

"*Tuesday, August* 15*th*, 1786, Contrary to all wont, the King did not awaken till 11 o'clock. On first looking up, he seemed in a confused state, but soon recovered himself; called in his Generals and Secretaries, who had been in waiting so long, and gave, with his old precision, the Orders wanted,— one to Rohdich, Commandant of Potsdam, about a Review of the troops there next day; Order minutely perfect, in knowledge of the ground, in foresight of what and how the evolutions were to be; which was accordingly performed on the morrow. The Cabinet work he went through with the like possession of himself, giving, on every point, his Three Clerks their directions, in a weak voice, yet with the old power of spirit,—dictated to one of them, among other things, an 'Instruction' for some Ambassador

just leaving; 'four quarto pages, which,' says Herzberg, 'would have done honour to the most experi-
enced Minister;' and, in the evening, he signed his
Missives as usual.   This evening still,—but—no
evening more.   We are now at the last scene of all,
which ends this strange eventful History.

"Wednesday morning, General-Adjutants, Secretaries, Commandant, were there at their old hours;
but word came out, 'Secretaries are to wait:' King
is in a kind of sleep, of stertorous ominous character, as if it were the death-sleep; seems not to recollect himself, when he does at intervals open his
eyes.   After hours of this, on a ray of consciousness, the King bethought him of Rohdich, the Commandant; tried to give Rohdich the Parole as usual;
tried twice, perhaps three times; but found he could
not speak;—and with a glance of sorrow, which
seemed to say, 'It is impossible, then!' turned his
head, and sank back into the corner of his chair.
Rohdich burst into tears: the King again lay slum-
berous;—the rattle of death beginning soon after,
which lasted at intervals all day.   Selle, in Berlin, was
sent for by express; he arrived about 3 of the afternoon: King seemed a little more conscious, knew
those about him, 'his face red rather than pale, in

his eyes still something of their old fire.' Towards evening the feverishness abated (to Selle, I suppose, a fatal symptom); the King fell into a soft sleep, with warm perspiration; but, on awakening, complained of cold, repeatedly of cold, demanding wrappage after wrappage (*'Kissen,'* soft *quilt* of the old fashion);—and on examining feet and legs, one of the Doctors made signs that they were in fact cold, up nearly to the knee. 'What said he of the feet?' murmured the King some time afterwards, the Doctor having now stepped out of sight. 'Much the same as before,' answered some attendant. The King shook his head, incredulous.

"He drank once, grasping the goblet with both hands, a draught of fennel-water, his customary drink; and seemed relieved by it;—his last reflection in this world. Towards nine in the evening, there had come on a continual short cough, and a rattling in the breast, breath more and more difficult. Why continue? Friedrich is making exit, on the common terms; you may *hear* the curtain rustling down. For most part he was unconscious, never more than half-conscious. As the wall-clock above his head struck 11, he asked: 'What o'clock?' 'Eleven,' answered they. 'At 4,' murmured he, 'I will rise.'

One of his dogs sat on its stool near him; about midnight he noticed it shivering for cold: 'Throw a quilt over it,' said or beckoned he; that, I think, was his last completely-conscious utterance. Afterwards, in a severe choking fit, getting at last rid of the phlegm, he said, *'La montagne est passée, nous irons mieux.* We are over the hill, we shall go better now.'

"Attendants, Herzberg, Selle and one or two others, were in the outer room; none in Friedrich's but Strützki, his Kammerhussar, one of Three who are his sole valets and nurses; a faithful ingenious man, as they all seem to be, and excellently chosen for the object; Strützki, to save the King from hustling down, as he always did, into the corner of his chair, where, with neck and chest bent forward, breathing was impossible,—at last took the King on his knee; kneeling on the ground with his other knee for the purpose,—King's right arm round Strützki's neck, Strützki's left arm round the King's back, and supporting his other shoulder; in which posture the faithful creature, for above two hours, sat motionless, till the end came. Within doors, all is silence, except this breathing; around it the dark earth silent, above it the silent stars. At 20 minutes past

2, the breathing paused,—wavered; ceased. Friedrich's Life-battle is fought out; instead of suffering and sore labour, here is now rest. Thursday morning 17th August 1786, at the dark hour just named. On the 31st of May last, this King had reigned 46 years. 'He has lived,' counts Rödenbeck, '74 years, 6 months and 24 days.'

"His death seems very stern and lonely;—a man of such affectionate feelings, too; 'a man with more sensibility than other men!' But so had his whole life been, stern and lonely; such the severe law laid on him. Nor was it inappropriate that he found his death in that poor Silesian Review; punctually doing, as usual, the work that had come in hand. Nor that he died now, rather than a few years later. In these final days of his, we have transiently noticed Arch-Cardinal de Rohan, Arch-Quack Cagliostro, and a most select Company of Persons and of Actions, like an Elixir of the Nether World, miraculously emerging into daylight; and all Paris, and by degrees all Europe, getting loud with the *Diamond-Necklace* History. And to eyes of deeper speculation,—World-Poet Goethe's, for instance,—it is becoming evident that Chaos is again big. As has not she proved to be, and is still proving, in the most

teeming way! Better for a Royal Hero, fallen old
and feeble, to be hidden from such things. . . .

"Friedrich was not buried at Sans-Souci, in the
Tomb which he had built for himself; why not, nobody clearly says. By his own express will, there
was no embalming. Two Regiment-surgeons
washed the Corpse, decently prepared it for inter-
ment: 'at 8 that same evening, Friedrich's Body,
dressed in the uniform of the First Battalion of
Guards, and laid in its coffin, was borne to Potsdam,
in a hearse of eight horses, twelve Non-commis-
sioned Officers of the Guard escorting. All Potsdam
was in the streets; the Soldiers, of their own accord,
formed rank, and followed the hearse; many a
rugged face unable to restrain tears: for the rest,
universal silence as of midnight, nothing audible
among the people but here and there a sob, and the
murmur, *"Ach, der gute König!"*

" 'All next day, the Body lay in state in the Palace;
thousands crowding, from Berlin and the other environs, to see that face for the last time. Wasted,
worn; but beautiful in death, with the thin gray hair
parted into locks, and slightly powdered. And at 8
in the evening' (Friday 18th), 'he was borne to the
Garnison-Kirche of Potsdam; and laid beside his

Father, in the vault behind the Pulpit there,'—where the two Coffins are still to be seen.

"I define him to myself as hitherto the Last of the Kings;—when the Next will be, is a very long question! But it seems to me as if Nations, probably all Nations, by and by, in their despair,—blinded, swallowed like Jonah, in such a whale's-belly of things brutish, waste, abominable (for is not Anarchy, or the Rule of what is Baser over what is Nobler, the one life's-misery worth complaining of, and, in fact, the abomination of abominations, springing from and producing all others whatsoever?)—as if the Nations universally, and England too if it hold on, may more and more bethink themselves of such a Man and his Function and Performance, with feelings far other than are possible at present. Meanwhile, all I had to say of him is finished: that too, it seems, was a bit of work appointed to be done. Adieu, good readers; bad also, adieu."

To one who knows Carlyle's work in its entirety and recognizes in his *Frederick the Great* the last Herculean labor of an intellect that had now spent its best strength, that sentence of adieu to good and bad readers alike makes the fittest close for this little book. No comment can add anything to its note of quiet pathos, or to its clear-eyed vision of the transiency of much of our human effort, the futility of many of our human hopes. The weary giant has done his work at last, for better or worse, and may rest now, even as his toiling stonemason father had done before him. "Let me write my books as he built his houses, and walk as blamelessly through this shadow world." That prayer of Carlyle's early manhood had been answered.

Yet how many Americans, in this first quarter of the twentieth century, may fairly be said to know Carlyle's work in its entirety, or, for that matter, the entire work of any of the great Victorians? The drift of our age is against such robust and masculine effort to grapple with the total output of any first-rate mind. We read by scraps and patches. We recall phrases, we retain impressionistic glimpses of characteristic attitudes and gestures, we hazard our facile American guess at the personality of a Thomas Carlyle, as we do at a hundred others of yesterday's distinguished names. This very book whose last page I am writing can not be expected to correct in the least degree this wide-spread temper of our age. But its intent, at any rate, has been to invite a new generation of hurried and pre-occupied Americans to look back steadily and wisely upon a great figure, and to study that figure in the light of Carlyle's own varied and stimulating and magnificent utterances. This book is not a substitute for a thorough knowledge of Thomas Carlyle. Yet it may help some readers to try to climb the mountain for themselves. The mountain is there—twenty-five matchless volumes of it!—and it may be climbed by any one possessing the strength and spirit of a mountaineer. There are shadows in its deep valleys, and they darken toward the evening, as all earthly shadows do; but one climbs this mountain not so much to watch the lengthening shadows as to see a sunrise lighting an illimitable world.

THE .END

INDEX

INDEX